Bullying
AND
Students with
Disabilities

Bullying

AND

Students with
Disabilities

Strategies and Techniques
To Create a Safe Learning
Environment for All

BARRY EDWARDS McNAMARA

CORWIN
A SAGE Company

CORWIN
A SAGE Company

FOR INFORMATION:

Corwin
A SAGE Company
2455 Teller Road
Thousand Oaks, California 91320
(800) 233–9936
www.corwin.com

SAGE Publications Ltd.
1 Oliver's Yard
55 City Road
London EC1Y 1SP
United Kingdom

SAGE Publications India Pvt. Ltd.
B 1/I 1 Mohan Cooperative Industrial Area
Mathura Road, New Delhi 110 044
India

SAGE Publications Asia-Pacific Pte. Ltd.
3 Church Street
#10–04 Samsung Hub
Singapore 049483

Printed in the United States of America

A catalog record of this book is available from the Library of Congress.

ISBN 978-1-4522-8318-0

Acquisitions Editor: Jessica Allan
Associate Editor: Kimberly Greenberg
Editorial Assistants: Heidi Arndt and
    Cesar Reyes
Project Editor: Amy Schroller
Copy Editor: Pam Schroeder
Typesetter: Hurix Systems Pvt. Ltd.
Proofreader: Laura Webb
Indexer: Maria Sosnowski
Cover Designer: Gail Buschman

This book is printed on acid-free paper.

MIX
Paper from
responsible sources
FSC® C014174

13 14 15 16 17 10 9 8 7 6 5 4 3 2 1

Contents

Acknowledgments

My work on this topic has been greatly influenced by parents of students who have been bullied in school and the victims themselves. Their willingness to share their experiences with me is very much appreciated.

Jessica Allan, Senior Acquisitions Editor at Corwin, has been remarkably responsive and supportive. She has provided valuable feedback throughout the entire process. I truly appreciate her advice and expertise.

This book is written in memory of my mother, Ursula McNamara, a woman of strong faith, who was optimistic and resilient—and quite a character! And it is dedicated to my grandchildren, Lucy and Logan. The world stops when I am with them. I find myself just staring at them, still amazed that I am their grandpa. Words cannot fully express the depths of my love for them. I also want to acknowledge the contributions of other members of my family. Much of my thinking on bullying is the result of collaboration with my wife, Fran. Together, we've written and spoken on the subject and worked directly with victims and their families. She has made invaluable contributions to this book, and her voice is present throughout. Her love and support have been reassuring constants in my life. I always know I can count on her to know exactly what I need, even before I know what I need. We are blessed with wonderful daughters, Melissa and Tracy. They have very busy, productive lives yet never fail to offer (and provide!) assistance to me. Their ongoing reinforcement, encouragement, and efforts on my behalf are very much appreciated. They exemplify the attributes of kindness, caring, and empathy in all they do. Finally, I want to acknowledge my son-in-law, Todd J. Hirsch, for his interest in and support of my work (and for Lucy and Logan!).

Publisher's Acknowledgments

Corwin gratefully acknowledges the contributions of the following reviewers:

Barbara Hayhurst, Special Education Teacher
Lakevue Elementary, Nampa, ID

Kelli S. Kercher, Special Education Team Leader
Murray City School District, Murray, UT

Mary Reeve, Educational Administrator
Gallup McKinley County Schools, Gallup, NM

About the Author

Dr. Barry Edwards McNamara is a Professor of Special Education at Dowling College in Oakdale, New York. He received his BA from St. Benedict's College, his MS Ed. from University of Kansas (Special Education: Learning Disabilities), and his doctorate from Columbia University's Teachers College in Special Education: Learning Disabilities. In addition to teaching at the college level, Dr. McNamara was a special education teacher in a self-contained classroom setting and a resource room. He was also a Learning Disability Teacher Consultant.

He has published widely in professional journals and other publications and is the author of a number of books. He is the coauthor (with his wife, Francine J. McNamara, MSW, LCSW-R) of *Keys to Parenting a Child With ADD* (2 editions), *Keys to Parenting a Child with a Learning Disability,* and *Keys to Dealing With Bullies.* He is the author of three textbooks in special education, including the most recent, *Learning Disabilities: Bridging the Gap Between Research and Classroom Practice* (2007), published by Pearson. The books on attention deficit disorder (ADD) and bullying were translated into Chinese. His textbook on the resource room was translated into Japanese, and the learning disabilities (LD) textbook was translated into Korean.

Dr. McNamara has made innumerable presentations to national, state, and local professional organizations and is a consultant to many school districts throughout the United States. His current consulting activities include developing and implementing coteaching programs for collaborative classes, developing and implementing behavioral interventions, and providing training on the identification and treatment of attention deficit hyperactivity disorder (ADHD).

He is also a frequent presenter on bullying at professional and parent organizations and serves as a consultant to schools on ways to implement school-wide bullying prevention programs that are accessible to all students.

1

What Is Bullying?

What Is Bullying?

Bullying! Even the word conjures up uncomfortable feelings in adults today who were victims of classroom or playground teasing, taunting, or physical aggression. What may have been considered benign name-calling in the past continues to manifest itself in painful ways for those students who are victimized. This is not a typical rite of passage. Rather, it is a serious issue deserving the intervention of adults. And while prevalence figures vary greatly, 20 to 30 percent of students are involved in bullying, either as a bully or a victim (Rose, Monda-Amaya, & Espelage, 2011).

Stop Bullying Now (n.d., stopbullying.gov), the U.S. Department of Health and Human Services National Bullying Prevention Program, defines *bullying* as aggressive behavior that is intentional and involves an imbalance of power or strength. It is generally repeated over time. The tactics bullies employ can be physical, verbal, intimidation, or exclusion. This type of bullying has been referred to as *tradition bullying*. Unfortunately, some students use technology to bully others, which is referred to as *cyberbullying*. Social media, the Internet, and simple cell phones (the most frequent tool used) can become devices whereby bullies can prey on their victims.

Bullies want power and are able to select their victims with uncanny precision. They prey on children and adolescents who are unpopular or vulnerable (Olweus, 1993; Carter & Spencer, 2006). The consequences of bullying can be devastating to students and their families. The fear, anxiety, and social isolation suffered by victims of bullying can result in loss of productivity in school and unknown psychological distress. Unfortunately, it can even be fatal. In one of the early cases that was highly publicized, a seventh-grade boy fatally shot himself because he was tired of being called "fatty" and "a walking dictionary." He shot one of his classmates to death right before he killed himself. Reportedly, his classmates said, "He was just someone to pick on." One does not have to search long for other examples. Hardly a week goes by when there is not a report in the media of a youngster who felt he or she had no other alternative other than suicide.

For these students, school is no longer a safe haven. They are fearful on the playground and going to and from classes. Even mild forms of verbal abuse have resulted in absences from school, lower grades, and overall anxiety. On top of the short- and long-term psychological damage is the damage caused by the failure of significant adults to intervene when they witness bullying behavior. Research and anecdotal information indicates that adults view the problem differently from students (Olweus & Limber, 1999).

There is general consensus as to the components of bullying. It is repetitive, there is an imbalance of power in the relationship between the bully and the victim, and there is unequal affect. Victims typically give in rapidly to the demands of the bully. This is the case of both traditional bullying and cyberbullying, where students bully through the use of technology and social media.

Who Are the Bullies?

What type of child would willingly inflict harm on others? The research findings are not entirely clear. Many researchers feel that bullies engage in this behavior because it makes them feel important. They may be insecure people who need to make themselves feel good by making others feel bad. Bullies achieve less academically, socially, economically, and occupationally. They are essentially school and job failures. Although not everybody agrees with these findings, they clearly represent the consensus of opinion on the characteristics of bullies (Wilson, 2004).

What does seem to be unanimous is the opinion that bullies are not born that way. They learn that being physically aggressive is a way to get what they want, a way to control people. Where do they learn this? Most experts point to parents and other role models. Bullies see their parents using physical force to get their way, so they emulate them. Many parents, for a host of reasons, do not use effective parenting techniques. When parents resort to being verbally and physically aggressive with their children, they risk teaching their children that bullying is an effective way to get what you want—especially if you are bigger and stronger. The research on modeling is very clear (Bandura & Walter, 1963; Bandura, 2002). Children learn that those who are bigger and stronger can exert physical force on others. Therefore, the more the child is verbally and physically reprimanded by his or her parents, the more likely he'll find someone more vulnerable on whom to take out his or her aggression. Moreover, most bullies remain bullies throughout their lives. It becomes a vicious cycle—bullies have children that they bully, and their children become highly aggressive and bully others. Some experts suggest that bullies also learn their behavior from inappropriate role models on television or in the movies. There is considerable debate over the effects of violence on television and in the movies on children's behavior. However, for children who are in homes where the parents are aggressive, this can only serve to reinforce this bullying type of behavior pattern (Drake, Pryce, & Telljohann, 2003). There are suggestions in the research that there are temperamental differences in children that make them prone to be bullies (Olweus, 2003). However, this is far outweighed by the other factors mentioned.

Bullies do not outgrow this behavior—it appears to be a characteristic that continues throughout adulthood. And, as they progress through the adult years, they are more likely to be involved with the criminal justice system, having more arrests and more convictions and tending to be more abusive to their spouses. The seriousness of the problem demands policy changes in schools (Young, Ne'eman, & Gelser, 2011).

Who Are the Victims?

Many of us have been in situations where we felt we were bullied. Infrequent, episodic experiences with a bully do not constitute victimization. However, that feeling that we experience may help us to identify with those children who must deal with bullies on a daily basis.

There are two types of victims: passive and provocative (Olweus, 1993). The passive victim is physically weak and doesn't fight back, whereas the provocative victim is more restless and irritable and frequently teases and picks on others. Many children with attention deficit hyperactivity disorder (ADHD) fall into this latter category. This type of victim appears to have poor impulse control, acts out, and then becomes a victim.

Consider Emily. She was an easy target. Diagnosed with ADHD, she was impulsive and hyperactive. She would frequently say exactly what was on her mind without any filtering. She did not mean to hurt people's feelings; she just could not help herself. Her parents did all the right things; she received counseling, received special education services in a resource room, and was on medication. Yet, it was readily apparent that her classmates did not accept her. They would tease her and taunt her and knew exactly how to get her upset. Frequently, due to her impulsivity, she would initiate the negative reaction. For example, she would tell another student, "Your hair looks terrible." The student would often respond, "Well, I think your sneakers are ugly," and Emily would cry. Her teachers would tell her that, if she did not start it, it would not end up this way—if she would only learn to "think before you talk." Many of her teachers felt Emily was a bully, saying hurtful things to her classmates. This is understandable. However, she is a classic provocative victim. And while these victims represent a small percentage of victims overall, they are most often students with disabilities.

You know these students. They engage in behaviors that annoy others (children and adults), tend to be irritable and restless, and maintain the conflict even when it is clear they've lost. That is one simple way to distinguish between bullies and provocative victims; they rarely come out on top. As noted earlier, there is an imbalance of power in the bully–victim relationship, and while this may not be readily apparent with provocative victims, it is here. I observed a student on the playground during recess who was critical of other students' abilities. During a kickball game, he told one classmate that "you can't kick," and the student replied, "I can't kick? You never get on base. Ever!" Joey cried and found a paraprofessional who was on the playground to complain to about the student who was "picking on" him. The paraprofessional knew Joey well. He did this every day. She dismissed his complaint and said, "If you just keep quiet, everything will be OK." That was the problem. Joey was impulsive and lacked social skills. He could not keep quiet. This made it nearly impossible to get along with others. However, he never intended to hurt anyone, never won a conflict, and did not understand the consequences of his behavior. Joey, diagnosed with ADHD, was a student with a learning disability and was a provocative victim who needed help. Unlike passive victims, it is hard for others to feel sorry for provocative victims. They feel that they bring it on themselves.

Victims tend to be weaker than bullies. They are also anxious and insecure children who tend to have poor social skills. These behaviors tend to set them apart from other youngsters in their classes, playgroups, or camps. Additionally, most victims have a difficult time making friends and sustaining friendships.

Not surprisingly, many victims are not motivated and lack an interest in school. And schools are where the majority of bullying incidents occur. Imagine what it would be like if you were constantly worrying about what someone might do to you. What if you were never quite sure when you turned a corner in the school or entered the lunchroom or went onto the playground if someone would be waiting to pick on you? All of your energy would be focused on the bullying, and therefore, school would not be an enjoyable place.

Victims also have disruptive academic performances due to constant bullying. They may develop school phobia and, therefore, have frequent absences. Many victims avoid the lunchroom because they are preyed upon by bullies who will force them to give them their lunch money or their food. Even at the time of day when most children can relax and get a break from academics, victims are troubled.

Michael, a third grader, is an example of this problem. He was bullied every day during lunchtime by the same child. This child would gather Michael's classmates around him on the playground and tease him about his physical appearance or clothing or being a "baby." Michael was not an aggressive child and had difficulty defending himself.

Victims are nonaggressive. They avoid confrontation at all costs and may cry when attacked. The bully identifies the victim, and the victim readily gives in to the demands of the bully, thereby making bullying very rewarding. These passive children are not able to deal with conflict in a productive way.

Victims' parents tend to be overprotective, and therefore, the children don't have many opportunities to practice conflict resolution. The low self-esteem, fear, and anxiety are reinforced so frequently that the pattern is difficult to break. Over time, victims begin to believe that they deserve this mistreatment. They lack the skills necessary to combat the problem and can become hopeless and even suicidal. The longer-term psychological effects of being bullied can be devastating (Will & Neufield, 2002; Carter & Spencer, 2006).

Schools and Bullying

Schools must do something about bullying. Most bullying occurs to students in transit to and from school and in the unstructured, unsupervised areas in and around schools. However, some victims cannot escape when they leave school through cruel e-mails and texts or the use of social media. Children report that they are called names when they wait for the school bus; some are jostled and have lunch taken away from them on the way to school; and others report that their lockers are broken into, lunch money stolen, and belongings destroyed. Students report that they eat alone because no one will sit with them. And when they go to recess, they stay in an isolated section of the schoolyard. These isolated sections of playgrounds, schoolyards, and hallways in schools become fertile ground for physical abuse of victims by bullies.

Many victims have a variety of physical and psychological ailments, such as fainting, vomiting, paralysis, hyperventilation, visual problems, headaches, stomachaches, and hysteria. They have frequent absences from school as a result of these ailments or out of sheer fear. These are directly related to the presence of bullies in their school. The view that this is typical child's play is changing somewhat but not fast enough. One of the most startling findings from the research on bullying is that victims of bullies feel that their schools didn't do anything about it. Most students feel that they do not have any person to go to if they are victimized (Atlas & Pepler, 1998; Lumsden, 2002; Crothers & Kolbert, 2004).

One middle school adolescent reported that a bully cut in front of him every day in the lunch line. When he told his teacher, the teacher told him to work it out. The same child was a victim of physical aggression in the classroom. Whenever his math teacher would write an example on the board, a bully would slap this child on the head. When the teacher turned around, the bully stopped. The victim told the teacher what had happened, and the teacher replied, "What can I do if I don't see it?" Not surprisingly, when the child's parents told him to tell the adult in charge that he's being picked on, he simply said, "Why? They don't do anything."

What Causes Bullying?

A group of children on a school bus called a child names every day. If they didn't comment on his clothes, they made fun of his physical appearance, his school performance, or his family. This had gone on for months with no intervention from the school. One day, the father of one of the "bullies" was waiting at the bus stop when the driver told him that his son was taunting a "special education child" every day. His father promptly asked his son if he did it; his son replied "yes," and his father proceeded to slap him in the face at least three times.

A group of Little Leaguers are playing a game on a pleasant sunny day in any particular neighborhood. A seven-year-old slides into second base and knocks the second-base player down, who gets hurt. Everybody is concerned, and fortunately, the child is not seriously hurt. On the way home, a mom looks at her son and says, "Great slide, Robert. Way to be aggressive out there!"

The principal called home today to tell Matthew's parents that he was involved in a fight. He appeared to start it and hit the kid so hard that his nose bled. After dinner, Mom, Dad, and Matthew discussed the incident, and all agreed he would try to avoid those confrontations in the future. As they were getting up from the table, the father, with a wink and a nod, said, "Guess you got a good shot in there."

You are in line at a grocery store. A toddler keeps grabbing the candy by the register, and the parent says, "Don't touch that." He continues. Finally, she slaps his hand, and the toddler cries. The parent gets more annoyed and tells him to stop crying. He continues. She takes him out of the food cart, holds him in her arms, and spanks the child, who continues to cry.

Two children are playing with a toy. A third child comes over and takes the toy away. Parents enter the scene. One parent tells her child, "Don't let him do that. Go over there, and take it away from him." The child doesn't respond. Now the parent gets even more annoyed. "You have to stick up for yourself. Go over there, and get your toy back." The child doesn't move but cries, and the parent looks defeated.

These examples are just a few in which it is clear that a message is being sent to a child: Might equals right. Aggression is valued. If you are bigger and stronger than someone, you can use physical force.

There is a difference in stating that "bullies are made, not born" rather than "it's the parent's fault." In the former statement, there is no attempt to blame parents. What is necessary is that parents of bullies recognize the powerful impact of their behavior on their children. When they act in an aggressive manner, their children will follow. When they reward aggression, their children will display this behavior. When they use verbal abuse and physical aggression toward their children, their children will find someone smaller and weaker than they to do the same. This is not a predisposed condition; rather, these are learned behaviors. There may be some small evidence that temperamental differences can also influence bullying, but the overwhelming findings from the research are that parents play the major role. Some children might also be influenced by the type of movies, television, games, and books they are exposed to. However, this is also related to family characteristics—bullies tend not to have too much structure in their lives, and their parents are not as involved as parents of children who are not bullies (Hanish & Guerra, 2000).

The first step is to recognize that this generational link has to be broken. This is not as easy as it appears because "standing up for oneself," "being aggressive," or "being in charge" are viewed as valuable attributes. Society also appears to be somewhat ambivalent regarding these traits. The overly aggressive person, whether it be in sports, politics, or business, is often held in high regard. Society needs to change this perception.

What About the Rest of the Students?

The majority of students do not engage in bullying directly, yet they play a critical role in maintaining the bully–victim relationship. Referred to as bystanders, witnesses, or observers, these are the students that must be taught to get involved. Assuming the 20 percent figure most often cited as the percentage of students involved as bullies or victims is correct, that leaves 80 percent of the school-age population. These students may be fearful that, if they say or do something, they will be the next victims (Coloroso, 2002). Or perhaps they told their parents or a teacher and were told to "mind their business" or "if it doesn't have anything to do with you, stay out of it." Or it may simply be a student who wants to help but doesn't know what to do.

Oftentimes, adults tell of their regret at not doing anything about a classmate being bullied. One teacher spoke eloquently about the guilt she has because she merely watched as, every day, the bullies in her classroom berated their classmate for being "fat." She didn't laugh or join in; she just sat there and did nothing. And to this day, she feels badly about her own behavior, and she has become a secondary victim. These students, the bystanders, need to learn how they play critical roles in reducing bullying in their classes and in their schools. Without such training, it will be impossible to reduce bullying.

Gender Differences

Boys tend to be the subject of more physical acts of aggression than of social isolation and alienation. However, the fact that the bullying tactics employed against boys are more observable may account for some of the disparity in the reporting of incidents. Girls are more often subject to victimization in ways that exclude them from their peer group, attempt to isolate them, and spread rumors about them.

The bullying tactics employed by girls tend to be more difficult to observe. Rather than physical aggression, the research shows that girls tend to engage in intimidation and social alienation, such as not inviting a specific child to a party and getting other children to do the same, encouraging others to stay away from a specific child, or never including her on a team. More severe forms include writing malicious notes, spreading rumors about someone's reputation, and instigating fights between the victims and others.

These types of bullying tactics may not be as apparent as the physical ones, but they are just as harmful. Some might argue that they are even more harmful because they are not as observable and, therefore, are likely to go on for longer periods of time.

As in the case with boys, where teachers and parents will discuss bullying with the phrase "Boys will be boys," it is not unusual to hear "Girls can be so vicious." Both statements are sexist and miss the point. The patterns of bullying may be different, but the effect remains the same. It's not a matter of which tactics are more "vicious" (whatever that means!) than others. It is rather simple. Children should feel safe at home and at school. Anything that interferes with that needs to be addressed. Labeling the tactics and interpreting the nature of the tactics prevent swift intervention.

Perhaps the most important aspect of looking at patterns is to recognize that bullying is widespread, and there are many ways in which a bully can victimize a child. There needs to be movement away from the classic bully to becoming aware of more subtle ways, including cyberbullying, in which children are victimized regardless of their gender. Espelage and Swearer (2004) recommend moving away from merely looking at statistical differences between boys and girls and focusing on the social and ecological context in which bullying occurs. This focus on individual characteristics appears to be more productive.

Prevalence

Prevalence figures vary a great deal. Part of the problem is the way in which information is obtained. Most often, it is self-reporting surveys, and that data can be skewed. Additionally, the definition of bullying is not clear, and acts of violence are lumped into one category. The National Association of School Psychologists consistently reports that one in seven children is involved in bullying. Olweus (1993) reported 15 percent, while others reported higher. Clearly, bullying is not going away. Moreover, in the following chapter, the prevalence figures regarding students with disabilities will be presented, and they are alarming.

Summary

This chapter discussed the nature of bullying in schools. Characteristics of bullies and their victims were described as well as issued related to causation, gender differences, and prevalence. Chapter 2 will focus on bullying and students with disabilities.

TEST YOURSELF

1. What are the characteristics of bullies?

2. What are the characteristics of victims?

3. What are the characteristics of bystanders?

4. What is the parent's role in bullying?

5. What causes bullying?

6. How prevalent is bullying?

2

Why Are Students With Disabilities Targeted?

It was pretty easy to get Adam upset. His eighth-grade classmates realized this early on in the school year and would call him names, mimic his obsessive behavior, and mispronounce is name. It was this last taunt that really got to him. Adam was diagnosed with Asperger's syndrome at the age of eight and has always been targeted because of his atypical behaviors. However, this year, it was intolerable. A group of students in his inclusion class would whisper "Adman" instead of "Adam." The teacher would not hear them, but she clearly heard Adam when he finally could no longer control himself and started screaming and crying. He was unable to compose himself. When his parents came to the school, he sat silently, not willing or able to tell them what happened. It wasn't until the teacher started to investigate the incident that she discovered this was going on every day since the beginning of school—right in front of her, right in front of his classmates. And no one stood up for him.

Adam is just one of the many students with disabilities who are victimized in our schools. In *Walk a Mile in their Shoes* (AbilityPath, 2011), parents of students with disabilities shared vivid recollections of their children being bullied. These included name-calling, isolation, and taunting.

Some examples are so heinous that it is painful to read them. One student was forced to eat dog food. Another was tied to the schoolyard fence with his hooded sweatshirt, and in another incident, students poured alcohol in a student's drink to the point where his parents were called to school because he was hallucinating. One student was so happy to be included on a Facebook page only to discover he was the subject of ridicule and was humiliated.

For many students with disabilities, the bullying goes on for years. Consider Peter. Throughout his elementary school years, he was constantly bullied. Classmates made fun of his reading ability, his inability to recall words, and the way he would stare off into space in the classroom. As he got older, he became taller than most of his classmates and appeared to have athletic ability. He made the middle-school basketball team, and it seemed like the sixth grade was going to be a good year. One weekend, a group of boys from the team made plans to go to a local fast-food restaurant but called Peter at the last minute to tell him the plans were changed. Disappointed and sad, his father wanted to change his mood and suggested going to that restaurant themselves. Imagine the pain Peter and his dad experienced when they entered the restaurant and saw the seven teammates having a wonderful time as they ate their hamburgers and French fries and enjoyed being out with their friends. Peter and his dad made a quick exit and drove home.

This ongoing victimization has taken a terrible toll on students. The feelings of isolation, lack of friendships, and depression are common. Some students feel they have no more options left and commit suicide (Kim & Leventhal, 2008; Klomek, Sourander, & Gould, 2011).

There is a very limited but emerging body of research that suggests that students with disabilities are more likely to be victims than their general education peers. In a review of the literature, Rose, Monda-Anaya, and Espelage (2011) note that incidence figures of victimization of students with disabilities are in excess of 50 percent. Parents of children with disabilities report higher rates, with parents of children diagnosed on the Autism Spectrum Disorder reporting figures as high as 80 percent (Heinrichs, 2003; AbilityPath, 2011).

It should be noted that there are many limitations with this body of research. For example, most studies rely on student self-reporting, and information provided in Chapter 4 will discuss the problems associated with collecting data from students with disabilities. Additionally, the definition of bullying varies among the studies. While it is generally agreed upon that bullying requires repetitive actions, some feel that one incident is sufficient to label it as bullying.

However, despite these limitations, what clearly emerges is a picture that indicates that students with disabilities are more likely to be bullied. There is also some evidence that students with disabilities may also engage in bullying at higher rates that their general education peers (Rose, Espelage, & Monda-Amaya, 2009).

The Nature of Disabilities

Why are students with disabilities more likely to be targeted? The most obvious reason is their vulnerability. It has been established that bullies select those students who are less likely to be able to defend themselves (Olweus, 1993). Depending on the specific disability, students may display a range of characteristics that their classmates prey upon. Bullying is all about power, and these students are frequently less powerful, either physically, intellectually, or emotionally. This puts them at greater risk than their general education classmates. Mishna (2003) notes that their disabilities and the risks for victimization compound their risk for academic, social, and emotional problems.

Students with disabilities may not comprehend the nature of bullying. They may misread social cues and not be able to attend and remember specific ways to deal with bullies. They may have been placed in special classes or special schools where they may not have benefitted from appropriate social models. Or if they were placed in a collaborative, inclusive classroom, it may not have been one that provided adequate training for the teachers or had ineffective and insufficient academic and behavior interventions.

When discussing the ways in which students with disabilities display characteristics that may be at high risk for victimization, there are a number of ways to categorize these traits and behaviors. You can distinguish between visible and invisible disabilities (Carter & Spencer, 2006) or mild, moderate, and severe disabilities. Some employ a non-categorical approach and view commonalities among students with disabilities. For example, students with intellectual disabilities and those with learning disabilities may have difficulty reading social cues or lack good memory skills. It is important to recognize those difficulties in an individual student rather than the specific classification. However, others will discuss the nature of bullying as it applies to each of the 13 classifications cited in the reauthorization of the Individuals with Disabilities Education Act (IDEA) of 2004. This book will employ a combination of these breakdowns, emphasizing general characteristics and identify specific disabilities when it is necessary to illustrate a specific area of concern. For example, many students with disabilities have difficulty attending to relevant stimuli and may not always be on task. However, for those students diagnosed with ADHD, this is a dominant feature of the disorder.

Classification of Students With Disabilities (Categorical Approach)

As stated above, IDEA provides definitions of each of the 13 disability categories (NICHCY, 2012). They are listed below:

1. **Autism** means a developmental disability significantly affecting verbal and nonverbal communication and social interaction, generally evident before age three, that adversely affects a child's educational performance. Other characteristics often associated with autism are repetitive activities and stereotyped movements, resistance to environmental change or change in daily routines, and unusual responses to sensory experiences. The term *autism* does not apply if the child's education performance is adversely affected primarily because the child has an emotional disturbance, as defined in Number 4 below.

   A child who shows the characteristics of autism after age three could be diagnosed as having autism if the criteria above are satisfied.

2. **Deaf-Blindness** means concomitant (simultaneous) hearing and visual impairments, the combination of which causes such severe communication and other developmental and educational needs that the child cannot be accommodated in special education programs solely for children with deafness or children with blindness.

3. **Deafness** means a hearing impairment so severe that a child is impaired in processing linguistic information through hearing, with or without amplification, that adversely affects a child's educational performance.

4. **Emotional Disturbance** means a condition exhibiting one or more of the following characteristics over a long period of time and to a marked degree that adversely affects a child's educational performance:

   a. An inability to learn that cannot be explained by intellectual, sensory, or health factors.

b. An inability to build or maintain satisfactory interpersonal relationships with peers and teachers.

c. Inappropriate types of behavior or feelings under normal circumstances.

d. A general pervasive mood of unhappiness or depression.

e. A tendency to develop physical symptoms or fears associated with personal or school problems.

The term *schizophrenia* does not apply to children who are socially maladjusted unless it is determined that they have an emotional disturbance.

5. **Hearing Impairment** means an impairment in hearing, whether permanent or fluctuating, that adversely affects a child's educational performance but is not included under the definition of *deafness.*

6. **Intellectual Disability** means significantly subaverage general intellectual functioning, existing concurrently (at the same time) with deficits in adaptive behavior and manifested during the developmental period, that adversely affects a child's educational performance.

7. **Multiple Disabilities** means concomitant (simultaneous) impairments (such as intellectual disability–blindness, intellectual disability–orthopedic impairment), the combination of which causes such severe educational needs that they cannot be accommodated in special education programs solely for one of the impairments. The term does not include deaf-blindness.

8. **Orthopedic Impairment** means a severe orthopedic impairment that adversely affects a child's educational performance. The term includes impairments caused by a congenital anomaly, impairments caused by diseases (e.g., poliomyelitis, bone tuberculosis), and impairments from other causes (e.g., cerebral palsy, amputations, and fractures or burns that cause contractures).

9. **Other Health Impairment (OHI)** means having limited strength, vitality, or alertness, including a heightened alertness to environmental stimuli, that results in limited alertness with respect to the educational environment, that does the following:

a. is due to chronic or acute health problems such as asthma, ADD or ADHD, diabetes, epilepsy, a heart condition, hemophilia, lead poisoning, leukemia, nephritis, rheumatic fever, sickle cell anemia, and Tourette syndrome.

b. adversely affects a child's educational performance.

10. **Specific Learning Disability (LD)** means a disorder in one or more of the basic psychological processes involved in understanding or in using language, spoken or written, that may manifest itself in the imperfect ability to listen, think, speak, read, write, spell, or do mathematical calculations. The term includes conditions such as perceptual disabilities, brain injury, minimal brain dysfunction, dyslexia, and developmental aphasia. The term does not include learning problems that are primarily the result of visual, hearing, or motor disabilities; of intellectual disability; of emotional disturbance; or of environmental, cultural, or economic disadvantage.

11. **Speech or Language Impairment** means a communication disorder such as stuttering, impaired articulation, a language impairment, or a voice impairment that adversely affects a child's education performance.

12. **Traumatic Brain Injury** means an acquired injury to the brain caused by an external physical force, resulting in total or partial functional disability or psychosocial impairment, or both, that adversely affects a child's educational performance. The term applies to open or closed head injuries resulting in impairments in one or more areas, such as cognition; language; memory; attention; reasoning; abstract thinking; judgment; problem solving; sensory, perceptual, and motor abilities; psychosocial behavior; physical functions; information processing; and speech.

    The term does not apply to brain injuries that are congenital or degenerative or to brain injuries induced by birth trauma.

13. **Visual Impairment Including Blindness** means an impairment in vision that, even with correction, adversely affects a child's educational performance. The term includes both partial sight and blindness.

Students diagnosed with ADHD can receive special education services under the category of OHI. Additionally, some students with ADHD also have a learning disability and can receive services under that category, and if the student with ADHD is classified as emotionally disturbed (ED), they can receive services under that category. LD and ED were selected as examples because approximately one third of students with learning disabilities also are diagnosed with ADHD (McNamara, 2007), and almost one fifth of ED students are also diagnosed with ADHD (University of Maryland Medical Center, 2011).

Non-Categorical Approach

Students with disabilities may have difficulty in the basic psychological processes that underlie learning, such as perception, attention, or memory. They may also have cognitive disabilities or speech and language disorders and may not have adequate social skills. Additionally, they will most likely perform below grade level in academic areas, especially language arts. Understanding how these difficulties impact on their performance, both in and out of the school setting, will enable school staff to be cognizant of the risks for victimization.

Figure 2.1 presents a list of these areas of concern and manifestations. This is not exhaustive, and there is considerable overlap. All of these make students with disabilities more likely to be victims. Students seize upon them due to their vulnerabilities. Any one area would make the student with disabilities stand out, but many students have difficulty in multiple areas. Additionally, the nature of disabilities in school is typically defined by academic performance, and the list of difficulties is endless.

Figure 2.1　Non-Categorical Disabilities and Manifestations in and out of School

Area of Difficulty	Modification
Perception	• Misinterpret visual clues • Misinterpret auditory clues • Misinterpret facial expressions • Misunderstand messages • Misread social situations • Cannot follow rules of a game • Appears confused, perplexed
Attention	• Impulsive • Focuses on irrelevant information • Appears to be ignoring others • Cannot stay on task • Makes comments that appear unrelated to topic • Loses interest in games and activities • Appears to be bored with others • Cannot maintain a conversation

(Continued)

Figure 2.1   (Continued)

Area of Difficulty	Modification
Memory	• Cannot remember rules of games • Forgets what to do • Cannot retrieve anti-bullying strategies from memory • Lacks organization • Difficulty with multistep problem solving
Cognition	• May not realize he or she is being bullied • May not understand the nature of bullying • Cannot express him- or herself adequately • Misunderstand others' motives • Difficulty with receptive and expressive language • May appear to be naïve and becomes an easy target
Speech or Language	• May not comprehend what others are saying • Cannot express him- or herself fluently • May say the "wrong" thing • Gets easily frustrated • May be aggressive because he or she cannot use language adequately • Articulation problems may make him or her the object of ridicule
Social Skills	• Misinterprets social cues • Does not understand social situations • Not sure what to do in specific situations • Does not interact or interacts poorly with classmates • Cannot read facial expressions • Hard time making friends
Academics	• Struggling in school • Poor grades • Frequent pullout • May need significant special education services • Difficulty with basic skills, that is, reading, writing, math • Lacks prerequisite skills in many academic areas, especially content areas • Cannot complete projects or assignments

Classroom Placements

Most students with disabilities spend the majority of their time in general education classrooms (Salend, 2008). There is evidence that effective collaborative programs can serve as protective factors for bullying, whereas those students who are in more restrictive environments (MREs), such as self-contained classes or special schools, are more at risk. Additionally, students with disabilities who are placed in a more restrictive environment are more likely to bully others than those in collaborative classes (Carter & Spencer, 2006; Rose et al., 2011).

Classroom placement is another reason why students with disabilities are more likely to be bullied. However, much more research must be undertaken to fully understand why this is a risk factor. It is not enough to be placed in a collaborative classroom in order to reduce this risk. And classroom placements rarely take this into consideration when making placements. However, it appears from the limited evidence that students who are educated in inclusive environments have exposure to a wide range of academic and social behavior and learn to accept their classmates as individuals. Cleary, there is much that can be done to make any environment positive and supportive (See Chapters 5 and 8 for specific information.)

Summary

This chapter discussed reasons why students with disabilities were more likely to be targeted for bullying. The nature of disabilities, including the specific classification in IDEA, was presented, as well as a non-categorical point of view, in order to provide an awareness of the potential risk factors. Finally, classroom placements from the least restrictive environment (LRE) to the most restrictive environment (MRE) were discussed.

TEST YOURSELF

1. What are some reasons students with disabilities are victimized?
2. What is the difference between a categorical and a non-categorical approach to special education?
3. What are the benefits of each when viewing the nature of bullying?
4. Why is the classroom placement a risk factor?

3

How to Identify Bullies and Their Victims

How to Identify Bullies

Most bullies are aggressive and want to be in charge. They tend to lack empathy and a sense of guilt. Bullies engage in a wide range of emotional or aggressive behaviors that range from mild, such as pushing or shoving another child, to severe, such as threatening someone with a weapon. However, it is more than just physical aggression. They also engage in acts of social alienation, such as gossiping to maliciously excluding someone from the group. Bullies are also verbally aggressive and may engage in name-calling and taunting as well as threats of violence. Finally, bullies may attempt to intimidate and humiliate others using social media and cyberbullying. Regardless of the act, the object is the same: to exert power over another individual (Olweus, 1993; Craig & Peppler, 2003).

A parent at a parent–teacher association meeting told a story that left everyone silent. When she was in the third grade, three girls would intimidate her. They threatened to hurt her and her family if she did not bring in something valuable for them every day. She complied. She brought in little things from her home that would not be missed, but she was running out of things. One day as she was leaving for school, her mother noticed that she appeared very upset. When her mother inquired, the girl told her about the threats and that she had run out of things to bring. Out of fear and desperation, she took her late grandmother's engagement ring from her mother's jewelry box. Her mother was aghast! She immediately went to the school where the principal resolved the problem and moved the girls to a different class, had them return all the objects, and contacted their parents. They were told that, if they even looked in the direction of the victim, they would all be suspended. The bullying stopped.

The notion that bullies have low self-esteem is a myth (Garrity, Jens, Porter, Sager, & Camille, 2004). They are typically rewarded for their bullying behaviors because most victims readily give in to their demands. They are very different from most children and adolescents. They tend to misinterpret others' behaviors. Researchers suggest that bullies process social information emotionally, and therefore, everything is perceived as a source of aggression. This, in turn, leads to the justification of their own aggressive behavior (Olweus, 1993, Heinrichs, 2003).

Some bullies may also be victims. Provocative victims, frequently students with ADHD, tend to be ineffective in their aggressive behavior. They may say or do something to annoy someone. They get upset rapidly, becoming oppositional and defiant, but they can't sustain this level of aggression and give up. Most often, these children are victims, but at times, because of the nature of their disorders, they may engage in what appears to be bullying behavior (Olweus, 1993; McNamara, 2007).

Gail was frequently called names because she attended a special class for students with special educational needs. Gail has been classified as a student with a learning disability, and she also has the diagnosis of ADHD. She hated going to school and frequently complained of stomachaches and headaches. When she was in school, she was usually in the nurse's office. At times, she would "fight back" by being verbally abusive to the students who teased her. However, she was no match for these children. She misunderstood nonverbal cues and always thought these children were talking about her. Whenever she tried to stop it, her techniques were ineffective.

Students with disabilities may also be bullies. As noted in the previous chapter, there is a body of evidence (see Rose et al., 2009) that finds they have higher rates of bullying than their general education peers. And while the reasons why this occurs is not entirely clear, there are implications for teachers, paraprofessionals, and parents of students with disabilities that will be discussed in subsequent chapters (5, 6, and 7).

Thomas was one of these students. Whenever he wanted something his classmates had, he simply grabbed it from them. If they resisted, he pulled harder. And if they really resisted, he hit them. He is currently in the second grade, and these incidents have occurred since preschool. His teacher was concerned and used the term *bully* with his parents. They were not happy! How could he be a bully? He was usually a victim. However, despite his low cognitive ability and poor social perception, he had become proficient in selecting the most vulnerable of his classmates in his self-contained class and doing to these students what others had done to him. His parents could not believe this. How could this happen? They were aware of the school's anti-bullying program and wanted to know why it was not working. They believed Thomas needed social skills training and more exposure to general education students who displayed appropriate behavior. Maybe if that was done, he would learn how to interact more appropriately. They were fully aware of his significant academic and social problems but were equally adamant that he was not a bully.

One of the hallmarks of bullying is the frequency of the negative behavior. There will always be conflicts that children must resolve, ranging from sharing to issues of fairness. Some teachers may misinterpret some of these behaviors as bullying. It is important to differentiate between inappropriate behavior and bullying. Figure 3.1 provides information on signs that a child might be a bully.

Figure 3.1   Signs That a Student Might Be a Bully

- Constant teasing of other children.
- Intimidating, making fun of, ridiculing others.
- Acts of physical aggression toward others.
- Picking on children smaller and weaker than themselves.
- Having strong needs to dominate and subdue other students to assert themselves with power and threat and to get their own way.
- Being hot-tempered, easily angered, or impulsive and having low frustration tolerance.
- Being generally oppositional, defiant, and aggressive toward adults (including teachers and parents) and possibly also frightening to adults.
- Being seen as tough and hardened and showing little empathy with students who are victimized.
- Not being anxious or insecure and typically having a relatively positive view of themselves (average or better-than-average self-esteem).
- Engaging at a relatively early age (as compared with their peers) in other antisocial behaviors.
- Being average, above, or below average in popularity among their classmates but often having support from at least a small number of peers.

Types of Victims

There are two types of victims: *passive* victims, who account for the largest number, and *provocative* victims (Olweus, 1993).

Passive Victims

Passive victims tend to be weaker and smaller than bullies; therefore, they are usually unable to defend themselves. Many of them respond by giving in to the bullies and frequently cry very easily. Because they yield so readily to bullying, they tend to be targeted over and over again. And, the frequency of incidents is a hallmark of bullying. These children and adolescents tend to be very anxious individuals who are insecure. They are afraid of being hurt and are ineffectual in "fighting back." Not surprisingly, these victims tend to have poor self-esteem and often give the impression that they are inadequate and will not retaliate.

Passive victims are not effective in the use of strategies employed to deflect bullying. They tend to lack the ability to use humor or verbal persuasion. In general, they lack the social skills necessary to get along with their peers in a mutually satisfying relationship.

Provocative Victims

Whereas passive victims are fairly easy to identify because of their observable behaviors, provocative victims are more difficult to recognize. They represent a small percentage of the number of victims. These are children who annoy other children. They may tease and irritate and not know when "enough is enough." Their provocative behavior frequently leads to altercations. They are not particularly good at "fighting back," either verbally or physically and wind up losing. Unfortunately, their behavior is frequently misinterpreted by adults who often remark that they deserve it. Some researchers have commented that provocative victims are often disliked by their teachers. Teachers may, unwittingly, give the message to the class that this type of child is a "pain in the neck" and gets what she or he deserves. Many of these students have been diagnosed with ADHD.

Early Identification

The key to resolving any problem is early identification. It is critical to be aware of these identifications at an early age. It is known that victims tend to be weaker (physically, intellectually, or emotionally) than their peers who are bullies. These students also tend to be somewhat

Figure 3.2　Signs a Student May Be a Victim

• Missing belongings	• Never or infrequently being invited to parties
• Not eating lunch	• Avoiding school activities, especially lunch or recess
• Torn clothing	
• Unexplained bruises	
• Illness	• Frequently being teased
• Temper outbursts	• Appearing anxious
• School problems	• Staying close to teachers or other adults during breaks
• Fear of going to school	
• Cutting classes	• Unhappy
• Isolation or staying in his or her room	• Mood shifts
	• Depressed
• Few or no friends	• Deterioration of schoolwork

shy and less aggressive. Teachers need to be aware of these character-istics because these students are at risk for being bullied.

Some children and adolescents who are victims lack age-appropri-ate social skills. If you notice that a student has a difficult time getting along with others, doesn't appear to understand the rules of social inter-action, or doesn't always "get it," then be aware. He or she may be at risk for being a victim. Figure 3.2 lists signs a student may be a victim.

The school nurse is an excellent source of information about any bully or victim problem. Students who are victimized in school make frequent visits to the school nurse. They may do this to avoid activities, especially during unstructured times of the day (lunch, recess, or dis-missal), or they may go there because of illness or perceived illnesses. There is an association between victimization and common health problems in young children. Children who were being bullied reported not sleeping well, had headaches and stomachaches, felt sad, and wet their beds. Given this information, it would be wise to consult with the school nurse and not merely discuss the situation as a case of avoid-ance and "trying to get out of things."

Assessing the Problem

Prior to the implementation of any bully-proof programs, there must be a needs assessment. You can develop your own for your school, or you can use one that is already available. Figure 3.3 provides a ques-tionnaire for your students. Once you evaluate the results, you can get a better picture of the nature of bullying in your school, how often it occurs, where it occurs, types of bullying, and so on. It is wise to use this type of instrument as a pre- and posttest in order to evaluate the effectiveness of the intervention employed.

Additionally, many students with disabilities will have difficulty completing a questionnaire. As you administer it to your students, you should be observing their ability to read, comprehend, and appreciate the nature of bullying. This will enable you to make the necessary modifications that will make the questionnaire (needs assessments) accessible to all students. (Chapters 4 and 5 will provide specific forms for this purpose.)

Figure 3.3   Bullying Questionnaire

Name: _____

Age:_____   Grade: _____

How safe do you feel in the following places? Please check.

	Safe	*Not Sure*	*Unsafe*
Classroom			
Hallways			
Bus			
Cafeteria			
Bathroom			
Lunchroom			
Playground			

What type(s) of bullying have you experienced? Please check.

Physical _____   Verbal _____   Other _____

Have you observed other students being bullied in school? Please check.

Yes _____   No _____

If yes, where did it happen?

_____

Have you been bullied in school?

Yes _____   No _____

(Continued)

Figure 3.3   (Continued)

How often? Please check.

Once per
week _____

Twice per
week _____

More than twice per
week _____

Who did you go to for help? Please check.

Adults _____   Friends _____   Other Students _____   No one _____

If you sought help, were they helpful? Please check.

Adults   Yes _____   No _____

Friends   Yes _____   No _____

Other Students   Yes _____   No _____

Have you ever bullied others?

Yes _____   No _____

How often? Please check.

Once per
week _____

Twice per
week _____

More than twice per
week _____

Please list any suggestions for dealing with bullies.

_____

_____

_____

_____

_____

_____

_____

_____

Once you have identified the nature of bullying in your school, you are ready to develop and implement a school-wide program. The focus of this book is to ensure that this program is truly school-wide and accessible to all students. The remaining chapters will provide information and resources that will enable you to do so.

Summary

This chapter discussed ways to identify bullies and their victims. Readers were provided with observable behaviors of bullies and their victims and high-frequency characteristics of each group. Two groups of victims were discussed with implications for students with disabilities. The notion that these students can also be bullies was also addressed. Finally, a sample needs assessment was provided.

TEST YOURSELF

1. What are the signs of bullying?
2. What are the types of victims?
3. How would you identify them?
4. Why is it important to assess the nature of bullying in your school?
5. What are the implications for students with disabilities?

4

Creating a School-Wide Program

Research indicates that the most effective program is one that is school-wide. Some states have passed laws that mandate training for all school personnel, administrators, teachers, paraprofessionals, clerical and custodial staff, bus drivers, and monitors and cafeteria workers. For example, in New York State, the Dignity for All Students Act (DASA) took effect in September 2012, and provides specific mandates for training all school personnel in harassment and bullying, and calls particular attention to those groups who have a high incidence of victims, such as students with disabilities. In the past, school-wide programs did not address all of the students, and this chapter will describe the major components of successful programs and specific ways to modify them so they provide a safe school environment for all students.

Components of an Effective Program to Reduce Bullying

The most effective anti-bullying program is a school-wide program developed through collaboration of the school and the community (Olweus, 1993; McNamara & McNamara, 1997). The goals of such a program are twofold:

1. To reduce, if not eliminate, the bully–victim problem in and out of school.
2. To prevent future bullying.

Victims need to feel safe in school, and bullies need to learn how to assert themselves in more socially acceptable ways.

All school personnel and community members need to become aware of the serious nature of bullying. One way to do this is to give students a questionnaire or needs assessment (such as the needs assessment in the previous chapter). Once schools have developed an awareness of the problem, they can then address it. Without such awareness, they will resort to ineffective, outdated interventions that have little, if any, chance of success.

Most school-wide programs have three major components:

1. Clear-cut rules.
2. Reinforcement for students who obey the rules.
3. Consequences for not following the rules.

These components must be supported by the entire school as well as by the community members. See Figure 4.1: What Makes an Effective Anti-Bullying Program.

Evidence-Based Programs

Some examples of evidenced-based, school-wide programs are listed below.

- Steps to Respect: Bullying Prevention for Elementary School (www.cfchildren.org/steps-to-respect.aspx)

Figure 4.1   What Makes an Effective Anti-Bullying Program?

- Clear definition of bullying.
- Consequences for bullies.
- Reinforcement for acts of kindness and caring.
- Ongoing staff development.
- Training for students.
- School-wide reinforcement program.
- Cooperation and collaboration between school and community.

This school-wide program starts with administrators examining their bullying policies and programs. Then, all adults in the school receive training. And finally, classroom lessons commence. Students learn how to make friends; recognize feelings; and recognize, refuse, and report bullying. There are three levels with 11 skill lessons per level. There is an implementation support kit, and the site provides research and evidence supporting the program.

- Second Step: Social Skills for Early Childhood–Grade 8 (www .cfchildren.org/second-step.aspx)

This program teaches core social-emotional skills such as empathy, emotion management, and problem solving. Students in kindergarten through Grade 5 are also provided with training in self-regulation, executive function skills, and skills for learning. This fully scripted program provides online training and support. The promotional materials state that it is aligned with Positive Behavioral Interventions and Support (PBIS) and Response to Intervention (RTI). Research findings are also provided.

- Bully-Proofing Your School
- (www.soprislearning.com/school-climate/bully-proofing-series)

The Bully-Proofing Series is a comprehensive approach to preventing bullying in schools. It provides a step-by-step approach that can be customized for a specific school. Particular emphasis is placed on the majority of students who are neither bullies nor victims. Their promotional material states that it has been proven to dramatically decrease violence and verbal abuse while increasing students' sense of safety.
Bully-Proofing provides four levels of programs:

Early Childhood. Promotes the growth of constructive social skills and deters bullying behaviors. The focus is on prevention.

Elementary. This level teaches students how to interact, understand friendships, and problem solve through compromise.

Middle School. This level focuses on the students' ability to manage and direct their own power for the common good.

High School. This level explores the components of power and influence and enables students to develop a positive learning environment.

This program also provides workshops to schools for professional development and program training. Research results are provided on the site.

- Olweus Bullying Prevention Program (OBPP) (www.violen cepreventionworks.org/public/index.page)

This program is designed for ages 5 to 15 but can be adapted for high school students. The stated goals are to improve peer relationships and make schools safer, more positive places for students to learn and develop. Specifically they are aimed at the following:

- Reducing existing bullying.
- Preventing new bullying problems.
- Achieving better peer relationships at school.

There is an extensive list of materials, including the Olweus bullying questionnaire, school-wide curriculum with CD-ROM and DVD, and teacher curriculum with CD-ROM and DVD. They recommend that the program be carried out with fidelity, and schools should use the guidance and expertise of a certified Olweus trainer. This program has been extensively studied, and the research findings are available on the site.

- Peaceful Schools (www.peacefulschools.com)

The mission of Peaceful Schools is to develop character and social skills and prevent acts of violence in the schools. The program on the elementary level is Peaceful People (K–8). It is a classroom-based character education program that promotes five core social skills: cooperation, assertion, responsibility, empathy, and self-control (CARES). Peaceful School coordinators present 30 to 40 minute segments to classrooms, with the teacher participating. Peaceful Readers (K–12) creates thematic units around children's literature. Coordinators can provide the program or train teachers to do so. On the secondary level (7–12), Promoting the Peace is based on the foundation established in the Peaceful People Program. It is an activities-based program. Also on the secondary level (6–8) is Please Stand Up!, which empowers youth to take a stand against violence through thought-provoking lessons, scenarios, and other learning material.

These school-wide programs are some examples of evidence-based programs. As research emerges, these may change, and clearly, others will be added to the list. The major premise of this book is that school-wide programs need to be modified in order to make them accessible to students with disabilities. However, you should always start with a program that can be supported by research. In order to keep current with the research on bullying, you can go to www. stop bullying.org for a list of evidence-based programs. Another useful site is www.nrepp.samhsa.gov. This is the national registry of evidence-based programs and practices for the Substance Abuse and Mental Health Services Administration. It is not exhaustive and does not endorse programs, but it is a valuable resource. Finally, PACER's National Bully Prevention Center (www.pacer.org/bullying) provides resources that are appropriate for all students, including students with disabilities. (See pacerkidsagainstbullying.org for elementary-level students and pacerteensagainstbullying.org for adolescents.)

The first step in implementing an anti-bullying program is to provide training for the school staff. As previously noted, many do not recognize the severity of the problem. Children who are bullied frequently reported that they couldn't depend on adults in authority positions to do anything about the problem. Therefore, the first step is to create awareness. Typically, bullying is much more pervasive than most teachers think. Research indicates a difference in perception between teachers and students. Once they recognize the nature of the problem, they are ready to learn how to deal with it.

Training should provide appropriate role models, intervention strategies, and support victims. Additionally, staff members can use literature or videos as supplements. Many books provide excellent examples of dealing with bullies, empathizing with victims, and instituting preventative strategies; there are videos that do the same (see www.stopbullying.gov). Chapter 5 will provide more specific information.

There are many programs on preventing school bullying (see list above), but not all are evidence based. What appears to be lacking is a school-wide program that addresses the unique needs of students with disabilities. The remainder of the chapter will discuss ways to develop and implement such a program.

Including All Students in a School-Wide Program

Michael, a middle-school student with a learning disability, was excited when he heard about the new program in his school to deal with bullies. He'd been a victim of bullies throughout his school years. They laughed at him when he read in class, they excluded him from projects, and they constantly called him hurtful names. In the past, he'd wanted to report these bullies, but he had difficulty explaining exactly what happened to him. Plus, it had to be in writing, and that was one of his major weaknesses. He was hopeful that this new program would finally help him find the best way to deal with bullies. Unfortunately, that never happened. The district developed a school-wide program with very specific guidelines. They included all the major components necessary for success. The only problem was that Michael's disability interfered with his ability to read and understand the material. Even the needs assessment overwhelmed him because it was long and difficult to read. This was just another example of his expectations being defeated.

Michael is not unique. Too often, school-wide programs do not meet the needs of students with disabilities. Raskauskas and Modell (2011) suggested that there needs to be considerable modifications if all students are to be included. Heinrichs (2003) also discussed ways to make a school-wide program more accessible to students with disabilities. The same principles and techniques teachers employ to modify academic and social-emotional programs in order to meet their students' needs can be applied to anti-bullying programs. The major components of a school-wide program will be examined and modifications provided so that students with disabilities can benefit.

Needs Assessment

Prior to implementing any program, it is important to assess the nature of bullying in your school (see the questionnaire in Chapter 3). Typically, students fill it out in order to find out how they feel about bullying in their school. You will be able to ascertain the frequency, places where it occurs most often, who students seek for help, and the like. It sounds simple. However, for students with disabilities, this very first step in the process can be fraught with difficulties. Some students may not be able to read it, some may not be able to attend that long, while others may require the use of a sign language interpreter, and still others may not have the intellectual ability to comprehend the questions. The list is endless. The task of modifying the entire questionnaire so that all students have access to it may appear insurmountable. However, with a systematic examination of the needs of your students and ways in which they learn best, you can make the necessary modifications for most, if not all, students.

The modifications to the needs assessment must be collaborative. Teachers, support personnel (reading, occupational therapists, and physical therapists, speech and language pathologists), special education teachers who have expertise in teaching students who are deaf or students who are blind, and school nurses should be included. Anybody who can provide information on what works best for the student should be part of the assessment. Questions that guide this process will include the following:

- Can the student read the questions?
- Can the student comprehend the questions?
- Does the student have adequate motor skills?
- Is the student's vision adequate? Does he or she need special consideration?
- Does the child need an interpreter for the deaf?
- How long can the student attend for this task?
- Does the student have the intellectual ability to understand the concept of bullying or victimization?

The more expertise you have in building, the more exhaustive the list will be. Also, staff will be able to share common characteristics of specific disabilities and how these will manifest themselves in the classroom. There will be overlap so that a variety of modifications can be applied to a variety of disabilities.

The following chart (Figure 4.2) provides some examples of ways you can modify the administration of the needs assessment. They are applicable to a range of students with disabilities, across categories, such as LDs, intellectual disabilities, speech and language disorders, hearing and vision impairments, autism spectrum disorders, and ADHD.

The student's responses may also need to be modified. The needs assessment provided in the previous chapter requires the student to check off boxes and write in responses. Although the written component is small, it may pose problems for some students. For example, a multiple-choice format might be appropriate for some students because they cannot express themselves in written form. Additionally, these students tend to become anxious when writing is required, and this will allay their anxiety and result in more reliable responses. Some students may need to point and select from a few pictures depicting bullying in order for them to give a true response. Some examples of ways to modify the response are presented in Figure 4.3 below. Once again, there is considerable overlap. The key is to ensure

Figure 4.2 Ways to Modify Administration of the Needs Assessment

Area of Difficulty	Modification
Reading	• Lower readability • Read to student • Use familiar pictures • Provide specific examples
Listening	• Provide a distraction-free environment • Use shorter sentences and single words • Check frequently for understanding • Use pictures with verbal input
Attention	• Administer it over time • Use a variety of people to present it, including parents • Administer it at the time of day the student is most attentive • Provide reinforcement for attending behaviors • Readminister it using a different language, examples, or cues
Comprehension	• Use a video presentation • Use a PowerPoint presentation • Employ concrete examples • Provide specific examples of bullying • Use real-life scenarios
Hearing	• Utilize an interpreter for the Deaf • Use a frequency modulated system • Administer it early in the day in short periods of time • Have a familiar person administer it (including parents) • Consult with an expert in the education of students who are Deaf or hearing impaired
Vision	• Use Braille • Provide large print • Utilize a text reader • Read it to the student • Check frequently for comprehension • Consult with an expert in the education of students who are blind or visually impaired

that the student has an opportunity to demonstrate his or her knowledge of the information being assessed.

Let's go through the administration of the needs assessment with a student who has difficulty reading materials on his grade level, is very concrete in his thinking, and does not do well with people he does not know well. At times, he has difficulty focusing and can get

Figure 4.3   Ways to Modify Student Response

Area of Difficulty	Modification
Handwriting and Written Expression	• Use multiple choice • Have someone record the student's responses • Accept oral responses • Let the student point to responses • Have the student draw a pictorial response • Tell a story about the response
Attention	• Administer over short periods of time • Have multiple adults interview students over time • Provide verbal choices • Provide picture choices
Hearing	• Utilize an interpreter for the Deaf • Provide a frequency modulated system • Administer it early in the day in short periods of time • Have a familiar person administer it (including parents) • Consult with an expert in the education of students who are Deaf or hearing impaired • Use small group "discussion"
Vision	• Use Braille • Provide large print • Utilize a text-reading machine • Read it to the student • Check frequently for comprehension • Consult with an expert in the education of students who are blind or visually impaired

distracted by external stimuli. Initially, he can usually attend to a task but cannot sustain that level of attention for more than 15 minutes. First of all, you will need to reduce the reading level of the material or read it to him. Reading it to him may not solve the problem because the language may be too complex. You can use pictures of your school, his friends and family, and familiar places. Reduce the complexity of the language, and check for understanding frequently. Do not attempt to administer it in one sitting. Rather, space it out over time with ample reinforcement for attending. Use short videos to represent the concept (see www.pacer.org or www.stopybullying.org or www.ncld.org), and employ examples that he will experience in a typical school day. The more examples, the more likely he will understand the concept. You may want to readminister the needs assessment to ensure reliable results. Chapter 5 provides checklists to keep track of the modifications needed for your students.

Once you have addressed the issues concerning the needs assessment and believe that it is an accurate representation of what the student knows about bullying in his or her school, you are ready to modify the content and deliver the program.

Differentiating Content and Delivery

The same principles that underlie differentiated instruction (Tomilson, 2006; Bender, 2007) are applicable to the presentation of the instructional component of a school-wide anti-bullying program. All students must have access to the curriculum. The major components of most programs include students learning to identify bullies, identify victims, and develop strategies for dealing with bullies. Students with disabilities will also need direct, explicit instruction on how to report incidents of bullying.

There are a number of instructional modifications you can make that will have a high probability of success. Good teachers do this every day. However, it appears that these techniques are not always applied to school-wide programs. In previous chapters, the nature of disabilities was discussed and why these students are frequently victimized. Therefore, it is critical that they have access to all of the information available to students whose ability to learn is not compromised. The first step in this process is assessing the learning. Gather as much information as possible regarding the student's disability and how it manifests in the classroom. You can talk to colleagues, collaborate with specialists, examine student records, and look at the Individual Education Plan (IEP).

There is a wealth of information available on most students with disabilities that will assist you in making the right match with the curriculum. Some will be obvious, such as a student who requires Braille, and others will be more subtle, such as the student diagnosed with an auditory processing disorder. Assessment is an ongoing process. You may try one approach only to be unsuccessful. However, the reasons why it did not work will help you narrow down your options.

Vary the Method of Presentation

Not all students learn the same way. You need to provide information to them based on their readiness, preferences, and abilities. Most instruction is multimodal (auditory, visual, kinesthetic, and tactile). However, you will find that, for students with disabilities, their preferences may be more pronounced. That is, they may have extreme difficulty listening (auditory) to a scenario regarding bullying but may respond favorably if that scenario is on video (visual) and perhaps even more so if it can be acted out in small groups where they can move around the room and manipulate objects (kinesthetic and tactile). This is not easy to do with every presentation, but the more you make small changes in the mode of presentation, the easier it becomes.

Use a Variety of Reading Material

There are so many books on bullying available to teachers. However, you must make sure you have books on various reading levels. For those students who have visual impairments, you can acquire books in Braille, you can get books on tape, and you can utilize the expertise of your district's assistive technology coordinator, who can help you acquire useful technological devices like a text reader that can "read" books for students. Many students who are Deaf have difficulty with reading material and may require lower-readability materials. This is certainly true for those students with learning disabilities, as reading disorders are one of the major deficits. Many teachers create their own books on social stories to depict instances of bullying. These are frequently used with students on the autism spectrum and students with intellectual disabilities. These can be enhanced with pictures of students and familiar places and situations. All of the above help reduce the problems associated with not being able to read or comprehend the printed page.

Vary the Level of Difficulty

Some students with disabilities may have intellectual or social difficulties that interfere with their ability to comprehend some of the concepts of bullying and victimization. You can provide tiered lessons (Tomilson, 1999) in order to make the curriculum available to these students. In tiered lessons, you can provide the typical anti-bullying program for the majority of the students, enriching activities that expand the concept for those who are reading for this type of instruction, and lower the conceptual level for those students with disabilities that require this modification. The presentation should be more concrete rather than abstract. You should draw from the student's typical experiences and their environment and reduce the complexity of your language. Pictures, videos, role-playing, and acting out scenarios are useful modifications. Many students will need frequent practice and repetition with these presentations. This is an ongoing process.

Teach Attending Skills

Many students with disabilities will have difficulty attending to task. Some, in particular those with learning disabilities or ADHD, may be able to focus initially but will have difficulty sustaining attention. In order to capture their attention, use novel presentations. Vary the presentation, be enthusiastic, and keep the lesson short. Other techniques that are useful for increasing students' ability to attend are these:

- Keep the pace of the lesson moving.
- Provide frequent reinforcement for attending behaviors
- Provide advanced organizers. "Today, we will be discussing bullying. First we will . . . then we will . . . and finally . . ."
- Focus on the most salient information.
- Avoid extraneous distractions.
- Provide opportunities for movement in the classroom.
- Check for comprehension frequently.
- Pair students with those who possess good attending skills.
- Work in pairs or small groups to keep them engaged.

Teach Memory Skills

Explicit direct instruction in memory strategies will increase the success of the school-wide anti-bullying program for students with disabilities. A well-organized, sequential presentation will help your students retain the content (input organization facilitates recall). The questions and prompts you use to check on understanding should be directly related to the presentation (referred to as *cued retrieval*). Therefore, if you discuss the six things a victim can do if he or she is being bullied, then your questions should be the same topic, such as, "What are the things you can do if you are being bullied?" This way, you will be able to ascertain whether they were able to process the information. At a later date, you can introduce higher-level thinking skills. Other ways to increase memory skills are listed below:

- Use mnemonics. There is a large body of evidence that finds the use of mnemonics is very effective (Mastropieri & Scruggs, 2011). One that is very effective for bulling is HA HA SO (this will be discussed more in Chapter 7). Each letter stands for a strategy for dealing with bullies:

H Help

A Assert Yourself

H Humor

A Avoid

S Self-Talk

O Own It

- Group information into meaningful categories *(chunking)*.
- Employ frequent checks for comprehension.
- Work in small groups or pairs.
- Have students share their strategies for memorizing material.
- Use graphic organizers.
- Role-play bullying situations.
- Use simulations.
- Employ frequent practices.
- Utilize storytelling.
- Present information in game format.

Maximize the Collaborative Classroom

Most students with disabilities spend the majority of their time in general education classes (McNamara, 2007). The most frequently used approaches are coteaching or collaborative classrooms. Friend and Cook (2013) describe six coteaching models:

- One Teach, One Observe
- Station Teaching
- Parallel Teaching
- Alternative Teaching
- Teaming
- One Teach, One Assist

The approaches that are most applicable to teaching students about bullying are station teaching and alternative teaching. Station teaching will allow you to divide the class into three heterogeneous groups and provide activities and instruction in different ways and on different levels. If you utilize the alternative teaching approach, you can work with a small group of students (this should not be just the students with disabilities) who may need preteaching of the concept or additional assistance. See Figures 4.4 and 4.5 for examples of these approaches. More detailed information is provided in Chapter 8.

Figure 4.4   Example of Station Teaching

Lesson: What Is Bullying (Grade 3)

Students will be provided with various examples of bullying. There will be three stations. Station 1 will have three printed scenarios at different reading levels depicting students being bullied. Station 2 will have videos of students talking about their experiences being bullied in school. Station 3 will be a teacher-led discussion of bullying. Stations 1 and 3 are teacher directed, and Station 2 is independent. Students will be divided into three heterogeneous groups and rotate through the stations for 20 minutes per station. Following the stations, there will be a whole group discussion of the students' experiences at the various stations.

Figure 4.5   Example of Alternative Teaching

Lesson: What Can You Do if You Are Being Bullied

It was determined that some of the students needed additional reinforcements of previously presented concepts. While one teacher reviewed strategies for dealing with bullies, the other teacher was in a corner of the classroom reviewing the most salient features of the general concept of bullying to shore up the students' comprehension. Once he felt that the students were ready (usually only 15 minutes), they joined the whole class They did not miss any critical information because one teacher was reviewing concepts in a more general way while the alternative group was provided with more explicit instruction.

Summary

This chapter discussed ways in which the school-wide program could be modified for students with disabilities. All components of the program, including the needs assessment, content, and delivery, must meet the students' specific learning needs. Examples of ways to modify these components were provided. The following chapter will discuss specific strategies that teachers can employ in their classrooms.

TEST YOURSELF

1. Why is it necessary to modify the school-wide program?

2. What are some ways in which you can modify the needs assessment?

3. What are some ways in which you can modify the content of the program?

4. What are some ways you can modify the delivery of the program?

5

What Every Teacher Must Do

All teachers of students with disabilities must be aware that their students are at greater risk of being bullied (Rose et al., 2011; Siebecker, Wang, Maag, Siebecher, & Frericks, 2012). Unfortunately, school-wide programs have not addressed the needs of this population (Raskauskas & Modell, 2011). Most schools have anti-bullying programs, and the amount of information available on the implementation of these programs is vast. The number of books on the topic of bullying is overwhelming, and the use of social media to address the problems of bullying is omnipresent. See Appendix A for resources on bullying for students. Yet, for students with disabilities, there is a dearth of information specifically addressing their needs and the implications for bullying prevention.

Consider these examples:

> Jake is diagnosed as autistic. He does not realize it when his classmates are making fun of him. He just thinks that they are his friends. They make fun of him on Facebook, they post unflattering pictures of him online, and they continue to ask him to do things in the classroom that make him look foolish. He doesn't even know he is a victim.
>
>
>
> *(Continued)*

(Continued)

Louise is diagnosed with ADHD. She is very impulsive and is constantly blurting out things in the classroom. Her responses to her teachers' questions appear unrelated to the question. Her classmates find this amusing and snicker at her responses. Louise doesn't understand why they laugh.

Everyone thinks it is funny whenever Lori mimics Alex's use of sign language, everyone except Sarah. Sarah knows that it is wrong to do this but is not sure what she should do. Sometimes, she looks directly at Lori and glares. Other times, she will just look at her textbook, and at other times, she is so filled with anger that she doesn't know what to do. Should she tell Alex? Should she tell her teacher? Does anyone else think that this is wrong? She befriended Alex, but that doesn't stop the cruel behavior. Finally, Sarah told her parents, who notified the school.

Jared is classified as intellectually disabled and is currently placed in a self-contained classroom. He really does not understand bullying. When the concept is explained to him, he is surprised that anyone would intentionally try to hurt someone else. Jared is not above an occasional negative comment toward his classmates, but he never means to hurt their feelings.

The assembly program on bullying was just over when Mr. Macklin, a special education teacher in an inclusion classroom, overheard one of the students, Marissa, comment that it was a waste of time. When he asked her why she felt that way, she told him that they have these programs all the time, but kids still bully her. Many of her classmates agreed with Marissa.

Teachers who work with students with disabilities can reduce bullying. They must model appropriate behaviors, such as empathy, kindness, and caring. The classroom environment must be warm and supportive, and there must be clear, consistent rules regarding how students treat each other. The classroom must be inclusive and welcoming. Frequently, victims are isolated and loners. Attention must be paid to those situations that allow the inappropriate isolation of victimized students (McNamara, 2007). This chapter will provide teachers with a number of strategies and techniques that will allow them to address this problem directly.

Know Your District's Policy

In the United States, 49 states have anti-bullying laws. The key components of those laws were identified by the U.S. Department of Education in December 2010 (www.stopbullying.gov):

1. Purpose Statement
2. Statement of Scope
3. Specification of Prohibited Conduct
4. Enumeration of Specific Characteristics
5. Development and Implementation of Local Education Agency (LEA) Policy
6. Components of LEA Policies
7. Review of Local Policies
8. Communication Plan
9. Training and Preventative Education
10. Transparency and Modeling
11. Statement of Right to Other Legal Recourse

Your district's policy and procedures will be based on your state's law. You must be cognizant of the policy and how it is implemented in your school. It is not unusual for a parent of a child who is bullied to inquire as to the school's policy on bullying, and you want to be prepared to respond. More importantly, you want to make sure that the policy that is stated is actually carried out. In some states, the law will identify those students who are most at risk for being victimized. For example, in New York State's DASA, students with disabilities are one of the groups of students who are at risk for bullying and harassment. It is up to the individual school district to develop and implement a program that is mandated by the state. However, there is usually a wide variety of ways to meet the requirements of the law. For students with disabilities, special educators (teachers and administrators) must collaborate with families to address their unique needs regarding bullying.

Modify the School-Wide Program

This is critical if the program is to be accessible to all students. Chapter 4 presented ways to modify the initial needs assessment for a variety of learners. The list included students who had difficulty in reading, listening, attention, comprehension, hearing, and vision. There were also ways to modify the manner in which the student responds. These modifications should be ongoing. Teachers should employ the diagnostic–prescriptive model employed by special educators for academic skill instruction. You can constantly modify instruction based upon the performance and needs of your students. Once you have an accurate picture of bullying in your setting, you can move on to providing instruction. Again, this is an ongoing task, especially considering the wide variety of students with disabilities and their specific needs. Using the information provided in Chapter 4, you can keep a record of the modifications that are necessary for each student. See Figures 5.1 and 5.2 on pages 51 and 52 for examples.

There are a variety of ways to implement bullying prevention programs. Some schools use commercially available programs. (See Chapter 4 for a list of evidence-based programs.) Others develop their own, and others use a combination of both, allowing teachers to pick and choose those they want to employ in their schools and classrooms. Some school districts hire consultants to provide training, while others utilize individuals within the district or school. The role of the teacher of students with disabilities is to make sure that the materials and information is appropriate for the needs of the students. This is something teachers do every day when they provide instruction in academic areas. Now it must be applied to the strategies and techniques employed in a bullying prevention program.

You can employ the same types of modifications you employ with the needs assessment as you do when providing instruction. You can also employ effective approaches, such as differentiated instruction, collaboration, positive behavioral supports, and social skills training (these will be presented in Chapters 7 and 8) in order to address specific student needs in a bullying prevention program.

Figure 5.1   Modifications Needed for Administration of Needs Assessment

Name: _____

Age: _____   **Grade:** _____

Area of Difficulty	*Modifications(s) Needed (Check Appropriate)*
____ **Reading**	____ Lower readability ____ Read to student ____ Use familiar pictures ____ Provide specific examples
____ **Listening**	____ Provide a distraction-free environment ____ Use shorter sentences and single words ____ Check frequently for understanding ____ Use pictures with verbal input
____ **Attention**	____ Administer it over time ____ Use a variety of people to present it, including parents ____ Administer it at the time of day the student is most attentive ____ Provide reinforcements for attending behaviors ____ Readminister it using different languages, examples, and cues
____ **Comprehension**	____ Use a video presentation ____ Use a PowerPoint presentation ____ Employ concrete examples ____ Provide specific examples of bullying ____ Use real-life scenarios
____ **Hearing**	____ Utilize an interpreter for the Deaf ____ Use a frequency modulated (FM) system ____ Administer it early in the day, in shorter periods of time ____ Have a familiar person administer it (including parents) ____ Consult with an expert in the education of students who are Deaf or hearing impaired
____ **Vision**	____ Use Braille ____ Use large print ____ Use a text reader ____ Read it to the student ____ Consult with an expert in the education of students who are Deaf or hearing impaired
____ **Other Modifications**	

Figure 5.2   Modifications Needed for Student Response

Name: _____

Age: _____   **Grade:** _____

Area of Difficulty	*Modifications(s) Needed (Check Appropriate)*
_____ **Handwriting and Written Expression**	_____ Use multiple choice _____ Have someone record the student's responses _____ Accept oral Responses _____ Have student point to responses _____ Have student draw a pictorial response _____ Tell a story about the response
_____ **Attention**	_____ Administer over short periods of time _____ Have multiple adults interview students over time _____ Provide verbal choices _____ Provide picture choices
_____ **Hearing**	_____ Utilize an interpreter for the Deaf _____ Use a Frequency Modulated system _____ Use small group discussion _____ Administer it early in the day in shorter periods of time _____ Have a familiar person administer it (including parents) _____ Consult with an expert in the education of students who are Deaf or hearing impaired
_____ **Vision**	_____ Use Braille _____ Use large print _____ Use a text-reading machine _____ Read it to the student _____ Consult with an expert in the education of students who are blind or visually impaired

Provide Instruction for Dealing With Bullies

Initially, students with disabilities need one specific way to deal with bullies. After they become competent in one way, you can introduce different techniques. However, to provide them with a number of ways to deal with bullies may be overwhelming. An effective strategy was developed by Garrity and colleagues (2000) as part of their Bully-Proofing Your School program.

They developed a simple mnemonic device, HA, HA, SO, to help students remember exactly what they can do if confronted with a bully. There is a large body of evidence to support the use of mnemonics for students with disabilities (Mastropieri & Scruggs, 2011). This is particularly effective for students who have difficulty with attention and memory. It is described below:

HA	*HA*	*SO*
Help	Humor	Self-Talk
Assert Yourself	Avoid	Own It

Help

Teachers must provide explicit instruction on exactly how their students can get help if they are being bullied. Some teachers suggest students send them an e-mail, put a note in their mailbox, ask their parents to notify the teacher, come in before or after school, and so on. Additionally, students need to know they can go to any adult to get help. They need to be reassured that the bully will not know that they told an adult. Everything must be done to insure anonymity. On the secondary level, it is easier because students can go to supportive personnel, such as a social worker, psychologist, or guidance counselor. A class-wide discussion may reveal ways to get help that you never thought of that students would find beneficial.

Assert Yourself

Two things students with disabilities can do to assert themselves are to speak up and say something to the bully. They can also stand tall, walk with their heads held high, have good eye contact, move at a swift pace, and know exactly where they are going. For many students with disabilities, this is difficult, however, because they have trouble understanding the social environment. They may not "read" a facial expression or tone of voice correctly, or they may be shy or anxious and need a great deal of practice. Even saying something to a bully can be difficult. The statement should be short and stated forcefully, such as "Stop it" or "Don't bully me," or "Cut it out!" If it is too long, it will not be effective. Frequent practice of what they will say, almost like a mantra, will enable the students to feel more comfortable when confronted by a bully.

Humor

There are students with disabilities who can use humor to deflect the impact of a bully, but this is rare. This is particularly difficult for students with learning disabilities, speech and language difficulties, intellectual disabilities, and those students on the autism spectrum. They may not understand the use of humor or know what is funny and what is not, and they may not know how to use humor appropriately. Couple this with the increased risk of victimization, and it can lead to the type of difficulty noted by Mishna (2004), where the victimization and the disability compound the problem. If a student can use humor, it can be effective. However, it may not be the best choice.

Avoid

Avoiding situations and settings where bullying occurs is an excellent idea as long as it does not interfere with a student's aspirations or abilities. For example, a student with disabilities was on the track team and was frequently bullied by other teammates. A student with ADHD was continually bullied by the other Cub Scouts in his den. And another student did not want to be a member of the History Club, even though he loved and excelled in the subject, because a few students picked on him. In all of these examples, the students should get help, and the school and scout leaders should address the issue of bullying. However, if there are situations where there are places in or around a school that are not well supervised or where bullies tend to congregate, then clearly, students should avoid these settings. Students need to know about the places that may be problematic and steer clear of them.

Self-Talk

Many students who are victims of bullies are anxious and may be under a great deal of stress. This is compounded by the presence of a disability. Their vulnerability makes them perfect targets. By using self-talk, they may be able to reduce this anxiety and not be obviously upset by the bully. Many teachers of students with disabilities provide instructions on how to "talk to yourself" to solve problems related to academic skill acquisition and test taking. The same procedures apply. Also, for those students who receive speech and language services, the speech-language pathologist can be a useful ally in teaching students this strategy. Students can learn to make comments to themselves that will allow them to think clearly and come up with a solution and to look calm and in control. For example, entering the school bus, your student notices a group of students who frequently tease him. He can say to himself, "I'll sit in the front of the bus near the driver, and he will be able to see if they do anything." Or, "I'll walk right by them and sit with my friend who is always nice to me." You should identify those situations where self-talk would be a good option and provide frequent practice.

Own It

Going along with the bully is referred to as *owning it*. You do not agree with the bully. You are merely gong along with him or her to diffuse the situation. It can take the power away from the bully because he or she realizes that the bullying does not affect the victim. For example, if a bully is making fun of your student's hat or any other article of clothing, an own-it response might be this: "You know, my mom said the same thing this morning," or "I know, I got dressed with the lights out." A student who was frequently taunted about her glasses used an own-it response and replied with a friendly, "I hate them too, but my dad made me get them." By going along with the bully, the student with disabilities may be able to reduce the reinforcement the bully typically gets from victimizing him or her.

This strategy may be confusing to some students with disabilities, especially those with intellectual disabilities and students on the autism spectrum. They may think in very concrete terms and not understand that you do not agree with the bully. They may also feel it is deceptive, that you are "lying," and that is wrong.

The above six strategies must be frequently practiced so that the student can select which they feel the most comfortable using and which are the most appropriate for the situation.

Garrity and colleagues (2000) recommend weekly meetings to review the HA HA SO strategies. As is the case with all strategies, knowing which one to use is crucial. Students with learning disabilities, students with intellectual disabilities, and students diagnosed with autism may be able to learn the strategy with mastery. However, they may not know what strategy to use in a particular situation. Use concrete, real-life situations to practice the strategies, and recognize that not all of these are necessary for every student. The goal is to provide them with options, with the knowledge that they can always get help from an adult. This is not something they should have to solve on their own. All school personnel must provide students with a safe environment conducive to learning.

Bully-Proofing Your Schools (Garrity et al., 2000) provides scenarios to use with different grade levels, and they are very useful. Some teachers construct their own based on the experiences of their students and bullying situations they've observed. You can also ask students for suggestions and put them in a suggestion box labeled HA, HA, SO and they can work on them whenever they have time (see Anchoring Activities in Chapter 8).

Consider these scenarios:

Every time the speech and language pathologist takes Jared to therapy, a few boys in the back of the room mimic his articulation problem. Other students say nothing.

Mia has difficulty with gross motor activities and can never keep up with her classmates as they run out to recess. By the time she finally catches up to them, they are choosing teams and she is left out—again.

Henry received a text message from Sam making fun of their classmate's errors in a little league game. He texted that Bill, who has a hearing impairment, was running around the bases when they were screaming at him to stop. He ran past his teammate at second base and was called out. Sam said that this was so funny and everybody in the stands was laughing so hard.

Sally was hardly ever invited to any parties. She was shy, a little withdrawn, and had difficulty academically. She was classified as a student with a learning disability in the third grade and received social skills training throughout her school years. Now in Grade 7, she felt isolated and sad about her lack of friends. So you can imagine how excited she was to be invited to a party over the weekend—and how upset she was to find out there never was a party. When she and her parents knocked on the door, the person answered and said, "Sorry, you must be mistaken. There is no party here." Her classmates could not wait until Monday to hear all about it. They texted her throughout the weekend asking her, "How was the party, Sally?" She never responded and did not tell her parents about the messages, but she said she wasn't feeling well on Monday and stayed home from school.

Richard was tormented on the school bus. Every day a group of boys taunted him about his hair, his clothes, his glasses—everything. One day when he could not take it anymore, he threw his metal lunchbox in their direction, and it hit one boy on his head. Richard was suspended.

In each of these scenarios, the classroom teacher could use the HA HA SO strategies. The class can be divided into groups of no more than four, and each can have a scenario or one that occurred in their own class to one of their classmates. The students can discuss which of these strategies would be the best for the student to use, the second best, or the worst. Or they can come up with one of their own. There is no right answer, but students must provide specific responses. For example, if they think help is the best solution, they must specify exactly how a student should get help. A response such as "He can ask to see the social worker," or "He can go in early for extra help," or "He can leave a note in the teacher's mailbox" are all acceptable. As they are provided with more of these opportunities, they will become more competent in applying the HA HA SO strategies to deal with bullying in the classroom and their school.

Create a Kind and Caring Classroom

Punishment alone is insufficient in reducing bullying (Ross, Horner, & Stiller, 2011; DASA, 2012). Students need to be taught and reinforced for engaging in acts of kindness and caring (McNamara, 2007). Start by compiling a list of kind and caring behaviors. Ask students to list those they think should be included. Reinforce those students who engage in these behaviors, and keep an ongoing record of these acts. Using basic applied behavior analysis techniques (Alberto & Troutman, 2013), such as verbal praise and token economies, you can easily implement such a program. Some teachers give out tickets that say "I was caught being kind and caring," while others keep a list of these behaviors on chart paper in the classroom, and anyone who observes a kind and caring behavior can add it to the list. A list of classroom rewards can be given when students reach a specified amount. The more the teacher models these behaviors and reinforces those students who engage in them, the higher the probability that they will increase. In some schools, the principal selects a few students who engaged in these acts, randomly selected from teacher nominations, and announces their names during the morning announcements. In some schools, these students are given a certificate or a bumper sticker for their parents' cars or some other tangible reinforcement.

Provide Resources for Your Students

There has been a proliferation of books, videos, and websites dealing with bullies. Very few focus on students with disabilities, but they can be modified. You can reduce the readability of the books, select a variety of videos (some are very short and can be useful for students with attention disorders), and select the most salient features from the websites to meet the needs of your students. These can be used to supplement your (modified) school-wide program. Teachers need to be selective and not overwhelm students with too much information that may confuse them. The approach has to be systematic, not one that merely selects a variety of resources without any overarching goal. Many students with disabilities have a difficult time discerning relevant from irrelevant information. (See Appendix B for a quick guide to useful websites cited throughout this book.)

They need to be guided through the bullying prevention program with the strategies and techniques that have a high probability of helping them deal with bullies.

The U.S. Department of Health and Human Services' website (www.stopbullying.gov) is an excellent source of information that can be used for students as well as for teachers' professional development. The videos are short and are a good resource for those students who have difficulty reading and comprehending print. AbilityPath (2011, www.abilitypath.org) compiled a guide for parents of students with disabilities and bullying, *Walk a Mile in Their Shoes,* which can also serve as a resource for teachers. Many states have websites that discuss their state laws and policies related to bullying and provide resources to schools (go to your Department of Education website). For example, New York State passed DASA in 2011 (implemented in 2012), and their website provides information on bullying and harassment for all students, with specific information for students with disabilities and cyberbullying (see www.p12.NYSED.gov/dignityact/).

Keep Up With the Best Practices

In addition to providing teachers with resources for their students, the sites noted above also provide valuable information that will keep you abreast of the professional literature, current practices, and research. Professional organizations such as the Council on Exceptional Children (www.cec.sped.org) and the National Center for Learning Disabilities (www.ncld.org) are constantly updating information regarding the best practices for students with disabilities and bullying. Most states require some type of professional development for staff regarding bullying. Try to advocate for including information on students with disabilities because that may be lacking. Additionally, there are professional conferences, workshops, parent–teacher association meetings, and so on, on the topic, and the more informed you are, the more effective you will be in selecting the appropriate intervention for your students.

Be a Presence in Your School

An adult authority figure is a critical component of any bully prevention program (Olweus, 1994). Be a presence in your school; walk the halls; go to the cafeteria and playground; and be outside your classroom as students enter, leave, and change classes. Being visible, interacting with students, and reinforcing those who are engaged in appropriate behaviors can be a protective factor for your students. This is especially true in those nonstructured, minimally supervised areas.

Mr. Lewis was very aware of these areas. He knew that most bullying occurred in those unstructured, less-supervised areas of the school. He also knew it happened frequently on the bus. So he made sure when he had the chance that he would go into the lunchroom, go to the playground at recess, check out the locker rooms and restrooms, and be present before and after school where the students congregated. He also initiated assigned seats on the bus and provided training for all the bus drivers and cafeteria workers as well as the paraprofessionals working in these areas. The more he walked around and the more he commented on the students who were well behaved, the fewer problems he observed. His mere presence and reinforcing behavior helped reduce bullying behaviors and increased appropriate behaviors—not all to be sure but an observable difference.

Collaborate With Families and the Community

Bullying is a societal problem that most often manifests itself in schools. Parents and community members can be valuable resources. They can provide you with information about what is occurring outside the school and interventions they believe are necessary. Parents of children with disabilities can take active roles in the needs assessment, even administering points of it to their children at home in a safe, natural environment They can report to you and keep you informed about the program implementation and its effectiveness. Most importantly, parents and community members need to see that the school is serious about this problem and values their input. Chapter 7 will provide information for parents of students with disabilities and what they can do to help their children with bullying.

Address Cyberbullying

Cyberbullying is the use of technology to bully others. Students can use a variety of technological devices, such as computers, cell phones, and social media like Facebook, YouTube, and Twitter to inflict harm on others. The technology is moving at such a rapid pace that it is difficult to keep up with it. An excellent resource for teachers is the Cyberbullying Research Center (n.d.) at Florida Atlantic University (www.cyberbullying.us). Dr. Sameer Hinduyo, the codirector of the center, notes that students with disabilities are particularly vulnerable to this type of bullying (AbilityPath, 2011). Most of this occurs outside of the school setting, but the impact is felt in school. In *Walk a Mile in Their Shoes* (AbilityPath, 2011), a mother talks about her son with disabilities being beaten by groups of students who put the incident on Facebook and YouTube. Another parent describes the heartbreak she experienced when she viewed her son with a disability on a Facebook page. He was so excited to be added as a "friend" on Facebook, and when his mother saw the page, she discovered that the only purpose was to tag him in pictures that ridiculed him. According to the Cyberbullying Research Center (www .cyberbullying.org), forty-nine states have policies on cyberbullying and or an Internet Safety Policy, and you need to be aware of it. This is not the traditional bullying that may go away when the student is away from school. It is endless. Some examples are listed below:

- Spreading rumors about others.
- Spreading lies about others.
- Assuming someone's identity and embarrassing him or her by sending videos, establishing websites or creating social media profiles that victimize him or her.
- Embarrassing, humiliating, making fun of, taunting, and teasing others through technology.
- Encouraging students with disabilities to participate in situations that will embarrass them or be harmful to them and sharing that with others. This is done without the student fully comprehending the nature of the situation.
- Using blogs and chat rooms to harass and bully others.

The role of the special educator is to make sure that students with disabilities understand exactly what cyberbullying is, how it is used, and what to do if they are victims. On the secondary level, students with disabilities must be aware of the consequences if they engage in this behavior unwittingly. Additional information on cyberbullying can be obtained from the Cyberbullying Research Center, noted above. It is an invaluable resource and is frequently updated. Chapter 7 will discuss ways that parents can monitor the use of technology and reduce the probability that their child with a disability will be the victim or the bully.

Summary

This chapter provided teachers of students with disabilities with strategies, techniques, and procedures they must utilize if they are to reduce bullying in their classrooms and schools. See the checklist (Figure 5.3) that follows to make sure you address all of these concerns.

Figure 5.3   What Every Teacher Must Do Checklist

Have You . . .

1. Become aware of your district's policy on bullying?
2. Modified the needs assessment?
3. Modified the school-wide program to meet the needs of your students?
4. Provided ongoing instruction on bullying?
5. Become a presence in your building?
6. Created a kind and caring classroom?
7. Kept abreast of the best practices regarding bullying?
8. Collaborated with parents and families?
9. Collaborated with community members?
10. Addressed cyberbullying?

TEST YOURSELF

1. What is your district's policy on bullying?

2. List some ways you can modify the needs assessment.

3. List some ways you can modify the student's responses.

4. Describe the mnemonic HA HA SO.

5. How can you create a kind and caring classroom?

6. List some resources on bullying for your students.

7. List some resources for teachers.

8. What is cyberbullying?

6

What Every
Paraprofessional
Should Know

You just started your job as a special education paraprofessional. You are assigned to assist in the lunchroom, and you notice that one of your students from the inclusion class is eating alone. What should you do? As you walk down a busy hallway in your school, you notice that a group of girls is taunting another girl. You are not sure if they are picking on her, and she does not appear to be bothered by this. What should you do? As the students are getting ready for dismissal, one of your students appears to be upset and on the verge of tears. When you ask him if he is all right, he tells you that the students on the bus constantly call him names—cruel names. What should you do? These are just a few examples that frequently occur in a typical day in the life of a special education paraprofessional. At times, the intervention seems obvious; other times, it's not so obvious. Dealing with bullying is just one of the important functions of a paraprofessional who is responsible for students with disabilities. And if the paraprofessional's role is one to one, then this is much more likely to be a major role. This chapter will discuss the role and responsibilities of the special education paraprofessional in the implementation of a bullying prevention program.

Consider the scenarios that follow. They represent a typical day in the life of a paraprofessional as he or she deals with bullying.

Ms. Torres starts her day on the school bus. She is matron because there are students with disabilities on the bus who need additional support. There have been bullying incidents, and parents have requested an additional adult to help monitor the situation. Her presence has reduced incidents, but they still occur. One day, she notices a young girl attempting to trip one of her students as he walks down the aisle. She reprimands the girl with a firm "stop that" and changes her seat. When she arrives at school, she reports the incident to the principal.

Whenever Michael is called on in his social studies class, the students snicker. He has difficulty retrieving words and is often disfluent. Despite repeated requests to avoid putting him in these difficult situations, the teacher persists. The students continue to laugh, and Michael puts his head down on the desk. As his one-to-one paraprofessional, Mr. Stone has had enough of this and reports the incidents to Michael's special education teacher. They decide to have a meeting with all of his teachers to review Michael's needs, recommend specific strategies and techniques, and address the bullying that he faces in many of their classrooms.

During lunchtime, Ms. Lira notices that no one eats with Amy. She sits alone, and all of her classmates sit at a different table. One day, Ms. Lira decides that something must be done, so she sits down with Amy. She starts a lively, highly animated conversation, but none of Amy's classmates seem to notice. The next day, she brings a game to play, and before she knows it, a few others join. Each day, more students want to sit at Amy's table and it becomes the place to be.

Every day at the end of lunchroom duty, Ms. Mara was exhausted. She was so tired of telling the kids to be nice to each other, to include everybody, to keep their voices down, and to sit still. Nothing ever changed. She decided to ask for help. A few teachers and the principal helped her start a simple reinforcement program. Every time a student displayed appropriate behavior—that is, they were kind to each other, included all of their classmates, and used appropriate language (and volume)—they received a ticket.

The table with the most tickets went to the playground for recess first, and at the end of the week, the table with the most tickets received a no-homework pass for a day, and the principal came to the cafeteria to let them know how proud he was of them. Ms. Mara also found that, the more she told the students how good they were, the more they displayed appropriate behaviors.

The playground was very hard to monitor during recess. It was a large area, and there were always physical confrontations. All of the paraprofessionals noticed that most of the students with disabilities were excluded from the activities and stayed away from the other students. They were concerned about this exclusion and decided to start a program called "everybody plays." There was a simple rule: If you asked to play any activity, no one could say no. If someone asked to play and was told no, that game stopped. No one played. They learned fast that, if everyone can't play, no one can play. They also asked teachers to encourage students with disabilities to join in and would go with them as they asked to play. These paraprofessionals also used high rates of verbal and nonverbal praise whenever they saw students including others. They also made sure to tell the teachers about the great strides the students made and how "everybody plays."

Whenever Mr. Roberts walked through the halls of his middle school, someone would say something to upset Alex, his student. As his one-to-one paraprofessional, he wanted to assist him, but he also wanted to give him some space. The students knew exactly what to say to upset Alex and then would laugh among themselves as Alex threw a tantrum. Mr. Roberts never said anything because he had to get to the next class, and Alex was always concerned about being late. However, this had to stop. He informed the classroom teachers about the incidents and let them know he might be late. They collaborated on solutions to this bullying. The first time any student said anything that would upset Alex, the student was brought directly to the office. It did not take long before the students realized there would be consequences for their behavior. Mr. Roberts realized that this was not going

(Continued)

(Continued)

to be enough. He went out of his way to find other students (the majority) who never said anything, and he praised them for their kindness and respect toward others. The more frequently he did this, the more he noticed a change in the hallways. And when a student did say something that would upset Alex, others would tell him to "cut it out."

No cell phones in class—that's the rule! Yet many students continued to check their phones throughout their classes. Ms. Lawson, Kara's one-to-one paraprofessional noticed that she looked in her bag, appearing to check her phone, and began to cry. They quickly went outside of the classroom, and Kara told her she kept getting humiliating text messages from her classmates. This had been going on for a week, but Kara did not know what to do. Kara said that, if she told her parents, they would take her phone away from her. Her parents warned her that this type of bullying, cyberbullying, happens most often through the use of cell phones. Now she knew they were right. Ms. Lawson reassured her that the school would solve the problem. She reported it to the teacher, who went directly to the principal, who began an investigation.

There has been a considerable increase in the use of paraprofessionals in special education (Bassity & Owens, n.d.). The U.S. Department of Education (2010) reported that more than 323, 000 are employed in these positions. Giangreco (2010) notes that the use of one-to-one special education paraprofessionals "has become an increasingly common response to support students with intellectual and other developmental disabilities in general education classrooms" (p. 1). These researchers and others (see Broer, Doyle, & Giangreco, 2005) have discussed the effectiveness of paraprofessionals in a variety of special education settings and cross disabilities. This chapter will focus on the current practices and address ways in which these individuals can contribute to an effective bullying prevention program, with the realization that this important line of research is critically important, given the reliance on these staff members (See Figure 6.1 for a What Every Paraprofessional Must Do Checklist.)

Figure 6.1   What Every Paraprofessional Must Do Checklist

Have You . . .

1. Become aware of the district's policy on bullying?
2. Been given a paraprofessional handbook?
3. Discussed the bully prevention program with your principal and teacher?
4. Reported incidents of bullying to the teacher?
5. Received training on ways to deal with bullying?
6. Reinforced acts of kindness and caring?

Roles and Responsibilities

Paraprofessionals are more likely to witness bullying than teachers. The first nationwide survey to include paraprofessionals was undertaken by the National Education Association (NEA, 2010). They surveyed 2,900 educational support professionals (ESP), including 959 paraprofessionals. The paraprofessional respondents reported the following:

- They frequently witnessed bullying.
- Many students reported bullying incidents to them.
- They believed it was their job to intervene.
- They need to be trained.

These findings underscore the need for paraprofessionals to h a clear understanding of the nature of the bullying prevention gram in their school and to receive adequate professional deve ment that will enable them to intervene in the appropriate consistent with school district policy.

The NEA provides a number of resources for paraprofessi regarding bullying (www.nea.org/neabullyfree) and suggests they can keep themselves informed on this subject:

- Seek input from other staff members who deal with yc dents.
- Request bullying prevention training, and ensure that professionals are invited to attend.
- Become involved in bullying prevention teams.

They also provide valuable tips for paraprofessionals U.S. Department of Education and the U.S. Department of I Human Services.

How to Intervene

✔ Learn about bullying, so you know what you're looking for.

✔ Learn what your school's consequences for bullies are and what supports for targets exist.

✔ When you see something, do something—be assertive and calm.

✔ Express strong disapproval of and stop bullying when it occurs.

✔ Start with verbal warnings. Use the name of the student who is bullying.

✔ Label the behavior as bullying, and refer to your school's anti-bullying rules and policies.

✔ During an incident, stand between the bully and target, blocking eye contact.

✔ Safeguard the target; ask, "Are you all right?"

✔ Address the bully, and advise of or initiate consequences for the behavior.

✔ Address bystanders, and advise how they might intervene next time; use the teachable moment.

✔ Do not argue with or try to convince the student who is bullying.

✔ Deal with all bullying incidents consistently, appropriate to the situation.

✔ Report incidents as required by your school's policy.

✔ Maintain your own log of bullying incidents.

✔ Talk to other school staff about what you've witnessed, so they are alert to possible retaliation during the balance of the school day.

How to Prevent

✔ Treat students the way you want to be treated and the way you want them to teach each other.

✔ Focus on developing empathy and respect.

✔ Use positive, nonverbal interactions—a smile, a nod, a thumbs-up, a high five, a pat on the back.

✔ Notice something positive the students do, and say something about it to them or someone else where they can hear it.

✔ Avoid physical forms of discipline or intimidation.

✔ Initiate conversations with students about bullying.

✔ Don't expect students to solve bullying incidents themselves; they lack the skills.

✔ Encourage students to report incidents of bullying to you and other adults.

✔ Ensure younger students know the difference between tattling and telling.

✔ Role-play with students on diffusing a bullying situation and engaging bystanders.

Source: U.S. Department of Education (2010) and U.S. Department of Health & Human Services (2010).

There will be marked variability in the needs and skill levels of special education paraprofessionals, and it can be helpful for them to assess their own skills. Once they have identified what they know and what they need to know, a meaningful, appropriate professional development program can be developed and implemented. See Figure 6.2 for a self-assessment checklist.

These intervention and prevention tips must be viewed within the context of a school-wide program. There is no place for unique or idiosyncratic interventions. There must be a consistent approach followed by all. That is why it is so important to clearly state the roles and responsibilities of the special education paraprofessional. Some school districts provide handbooks for professional training and include paraprofessionals in collaborative team meetings. The goal is to provide a consistent program that is consistent with the state law and district policy. The responsibilities may vary based on where you are. According to a report on the role of the special education paraprofessional, geographic location may dictate your job descriptions (Spense Fact Sheet, 2001). If you work in the Southeast region of the United States, you will be significantly more likely to provide personal care and health services than in other regions. Across all

Figure 6.2   Special Education Paraeducator Self-Assessment

1. Can I identify students with disabilities who bully?
2. Can I identify students who are victims?
3. Can I identify the bystanders?
4. Do I know what to do if I observe verbal bullying?
5. Do I know what to do if I observe physical bullying?
6. Do I know how to use praise with students?
7. Do I know who I should report bullying to?
8. Do I know what to do if I am suspicious of a bullying situation?
9. What kind of information would help me perform better in my role in the bully prevention program?
10. What would be the best way for me to receive training (such as workshops, lectures, videos, books, etc.)?

regions, the organization found that most spent at least 10 percent of their day engaged in the following:

- Providing instructional support in small groups.
- Providing one-on-one instruction.
- Modifying materials.
- Implementing behavior management plans.
- Monitoring hallways, study halls, and so on.
- Meeting with teachers.
- Collecting data on students.
- Providing personal care assistance.

As previously noted, the one-to-one special education paraprofessional is increasingly being used in schools (Giangreco, 2010). They are primarily used to provide support for students with disabilities in classroom settings. Giangreco (2010) challenges this model based on five areas of concern: 1) the lack of data, 2) flaws in the concept, 3) inadvertent destructive efforts, 4) inadequate decision-making approaches, and 5) delays in attention to important changes. He urges the field "to find new and better ways of supporting students with full range of disabilities in inclusive classrooms" (p. 9–10). This article is particularly relevant to the issues related to bullying. If the individual's roles and responsibilities include protecting his or her student from bullying, then there must be substantial training, the same type of training often staff members receive. It must be thorough, ongoing, and not merely a one-day workshop. Additionally, the teacher cannot abdicate his or her responsibility for ensuring safe school environments for all students because a particular student, or students, is working so closely with a paraprofessional.

Paraprofessional Handbook

All districts should provide newly employed special education paraprofessionals with handbooks with all the information they need to carry out their jobs successfully. An excellent example is *The Special Education Paraprofessional Handbook* developed by the Hermantown School District, Hermantown, MN (2010). It is divided into five sections:

1. District Resources
2. Roles and Responsibilities
3. Special Services Information

4. Modifications and Adaptations
5. Resources

The section on roles and responsibilities is comprehensive. Of particular interest are the duties the paraprofessional may and may not perform (p. 15). The following list illustrates instructional roles and tasks that could be assigned to paraprofessionals:

- Assist individual students in performing activities initiated by the teachers.
- Supervise children in the hallway, lunchroom, and playground.
- Assist in monitoring supplementary work and independent study.
- Reinforce learning in small groups or with individuals, while the teacher works with others students.
- Provide assistance with individualized, programmed materials.
- Assist in the preparation or production of instructional materials outlined by the teacher (i.e., making picture cards, schedules, photocopying, etc.).
- Assist the teacher in observing, recording, and charting behavior.
- Assist the teacher with crisis problems and behavior management.
- Carry out instructional programs designed by the teacher.
- Work with the teacher to develop classroom schedules.
- Carry out tutoring activities designed by the teacher.
- Operate and maintain classroom equipment, including computers, smart boards, and augmentative communication devices.

In order to ensure legal and ethical requirements regarding the delivery of general and special education instruction, the following tasks are considered the responsibility of general and special education teachers and should not be expected of a paraprofessional:

- Be solely responsible for a classroom or a professional service.
- Be responsible for the diagnostic functions of the classroom.
- Be responsible for preparing lesson plans and initiating instruction.
- Be responsible for assigning grades to students.
- Be used as substitute or certified teachers unless he or she possesses the appropriate substitute teacher certificate and is hired as a substitute.
- Assume full responsibility for supervising assemblies or field trips.

- Assume full responsibility for supervising and planning activities.
- Take children to clinic, dental, or medical appointments unless permission is granted by authorized personnel.
- Prescribe educational activities and material for children.

Roles and Responsibilities in Bullying Prevention and Intervention

The paraprofessional can function as the "eyes and ears" of the teacher in those settings where bullying is most likely to occur. They are responsible for assisting in the lunchroom, recess, playground, hallway, school bus, and student pick-up and drop-off area. All of these are places where there is minimal supervision and less teacher presence. This is a great deal of responsibility as the paraprofessional is typically the first line of defense. An interesting study was conducted by Broer, Doyle, and Giangreco (2005). They interviewed 16 young adults with intellectual disabilities regarding their experiences with paraprofessionals in inclusive settings. The researchers found four themes emerging from these interviews (mother, friend, protector, and primary teacher). One finding specifically related to bullying was illuminating. Eleven of the 16 students were bullied. The bullying occurred in the typical places: those minimally supervised areas outside of the classroom. Those students stated that adults were not aware of the extent of the bullying. Those students that felt that they were supported identified the paraprofessional as the "protector." They said they felt safer when the paraprofessional was around. Clearly, the number of students is a limitation, but the message should not be lost on the important role paraprofessionals fill. Also, gathering first-hand information from students who experience bullying needs to be continual as it has important implications for ways to prevent and intervene in bullying situations.

Paraprofessionals need to know how to report bullying, who to report it to, and any follow-up that is necessary. They can also provide valuable information to teachers and administrators regarding the nature of bullying in the school. Specifically, they can collect data on the frequency and type of bullying, the effectiveness of strategies and techniques employed by students, and suggestions for prevention. All of this is essential for an effective program. This information can assist in modifying the school-wide program to meet the needs of students with disabilities. The following are some

suggestions for paraprofessionals participating in a bullying prevention program:

- Report all incidents of bullying, including cyberbullying.
- Be aware of the specific places where bullying occurs.
- Know what strategies and techniques your students use. Are
  they effective?
- Are there additional strategies or techniques they should be
  using?
- Use the same language (vocabulary) as your teacher.
- Reinforce all acts of kindness and caring.

Each one will be discussed more fully below.

1. Report all incidents of bullying, including cyberbullying. In
your district's policy on bullying and harassment, there will be definitions of bullies, victims, and bystanders (see Chapters 1 and 2 of
this book). If you are not sure, seek clarification from your teacher.
However, it is wise to report incidents of bullying even if you are
merely suspicious that bullying has taken place. Try to keep track of
incidents as data collection is a crucial component of an effective program. This is not meant to suggest that you have to follow the official
reporting procedures if you are suspicious, but at the very least, share
the information with the teacher or principal.

2. Be aware of the specific places where bullying occurs. It has
been reported that bullying occurs in those settings that are minimally supervised—the precise areas that paraprofessionals are
assigned. However, there might be other settings, such as a particular
corridor or stairwell or outside a particular classroom. Identification
of these places will allow administrators to deploy staff in a more
efficient manner. In one middle school, it was discovered that, when
classes were changing, one section of a school wing was an area of
concern. For reasons unknown, students were taunting other students at a higher rate than in other wings, despite the presence of a
teacher. By placing more adults in that wing, they were able to make
it a safe place for all students.

3. Know what strategies and techniques your students use. Are
they effective? It is assumed that your teacher will use a specific
approach and students have been taught when and how to use it.
Which ones are they using most often? Do they appear confused as
to what to do? Do they avoid bullies? Or do they request your help
when confronted? How effective are the strategies or techniques
that they employ? By collecting data on the types of strategies or

techniques and their effectiveness, you will be able to provide your teacher with valuable information that will enable him or her to modify the program to meet the specific needs of your students.

4.   Are there additional strategies or techniques they should be using? You have observed that some of your students readily give in to the bully, while others use ineffective techniques. Still others need more help when the bully teases them. All of these observations are important to share with your teacher. The more information you share and the sooner you do it, the more likely the students' needs will be met. The teacher may decide to work on a specific strategy for a longer period of time or practice more frequently or reduce the complexity of the instruction. Without this valuable input, the program will be ineffective.

5.   Use the same language (vocabulary) as the teacher. Students with disabilities may have difficulty with attention and memory and have difficulty remembering exactly what they should be doing in a bullying conflict. The special education teacher will provide instruction appropriate to their needs in order to increase the probability of mastery. This will be enhanced if everyone uses the same language, the same terms, and the same vocabulary. Therefore, if your teacher uses the HA HA SO strategy (see Chapter 4), you must use the same exact language. Providing students with variations and a number of options will only serve to confuse them. Carry out the program exactly the way it was taught.

6.   Reinforce all acts of kindness and caring. Whenever students engage in appropriate behaviors, they should be praised, and this includes acts of kindness and caring. If you are walking down the hall and notice a student helping another student with his or her locker, praise that student. If you see a student sharing his or her snack or letting someone borrow paper or a pencil, let that student know that you noticed how kind he or she was or that "it was very kind of you to do that." Students will appreciate any comment that lets them know you notice when they treat others in a kind, caring, and respectful manner.

Some adults find this a little awkward and unnatural. However, once you observe the results and practice you will become convinced that praise is an effective component in a bullying prevention program. Below are some guidelines for using praise:

1.   Make a list of all acts of kindness and caring, behaviors you observe in all of your settings. It doesn't matter how small (picking up a napkin on the cafeteria floor) or big (including a student who is always excluded in a game). The more you notice these acts, the more likely you will be able to reinforce them.

2. Initially, praise should be delivered frequently in order to establish the described behavior (Salend, 2008; Alberto & Troutman, 20013). Try to vary your positive comments, so you are not continually saying "good." It is helpful to be specific with praise. For example, "That was very kind to include Adam in your game" or "I am going to let your teacher know how you always make room for other students at the lunchroom table." Nonverbal praise, such as smiles, high fives, winks, and so on, also serve to reinforce appropriate behavior.

3. Praise should be delivered immediately after the behavior occurs in the early stages. Over time, you can reduce the immediacy once the behavior has been clearly established.

4. If you find it difficult catching them when they are good, you can post reminders to yourself in a book or on a clipboard or in your pocket—anywhere that can serve to make you more conscious of the need for praise. You can also keep track of the number of times you praise students. Some paraprofessionals keep tally checks on an index card, while others use rubber bands on their wrists, and others move chips (bingo, poker, markers, etc.) from one pocket to another. If you are very brave, you can ask a coworker to count the number of praise statements you use in a particular time period.

Confidentiality

Paraprofessionals must follow the rules of confidentiality. This is paramount when working with students with disabilities. Parents of these students share so much of their lives with professionals, and they deserve to have that information treated with the trust they expect and deserve. In addition to any direct information on your students, you will hear other information that should never be shared with others. In the bully–victim situation, you may have information on students and their families that should be treated professionally and with confidentiality. Your students and their families have the expectation of privacy as well as legal protections. The Hermantown School District, Hermantown, MN (2010), discusses this in a detailed manner and asks the special education paraprofessional the following:

- What information would you want discussed with others regarding your child?
- What would you like shared about yourself or your family?

- What would you like said about your family, your values, and your lifestyle?

They also list Confidentiality Pointers (p. 9–10):

- Avoid using names if you are asked about your job.
- Suggest that questions about students are best directed to the building principal.
- Do not share other students' names or information regarding their programs with parents during IEP meetings, conferences, or informal conversations.
- Information regarding specific students and programs should not be shared in the lunchroom, staff room, office areas, out in the community, or in any other setting.
- When conferencing or writing information regarding a student or family that contains confidential information, be aware of those around you who may be within hearing distance. Look for a more private place within the school building.
- No matter who asks you a question about a student, if you are unsure whether you should answer, don't. You can do this gently and politely. Remember that only staff who has a need to know should be given information about a student.
- For consistency of program as well as confidentiality, paraprofessionals must support teacher techniques, materials, and methods, especially in the presence of students, parents, and other staff. Questions should be directed to the specific teacher privately.

These are excellent suggestions that will serve you well in your position. The consequences for a violation of confidentiality are a loss of trust and respect from your students and their families. And it may even cost you your job.

Summary

This chapter focused on the important function the special education paraprofessional plays in any bullying prevention program. Roles and responsibilities were discussed as well as specific topics for intervention and prevention. Finally, the importance of confidentiality was addressed.

TEST YOURSELF

1. How are special education professionals involved in the bullying prevention program?

2. What are some roles and responsibilities of the special education paraprofessional?

3. What are topics that should be included in a special education paraprofessional handbook?

4. Discuss the use of verbal and nonverbal praise in a bullying prevention program.

5. Why is confidentiality so important in your role as a special education paraprofessional?

7

What Every Parent Should Know

If you are a parent of a student with a disability, you know that bullying is a problem. Despite the limited research on the topic, this is something you live with on a daily basis. This is not to suggest that all students with disabilities are involved in bullying, as a victim or as a bully. However, it is naïve to ignore the high prevalence figures and anecdotal information from parents and teachers. At the very least, your children are at a higher risk for being targeted as victims, and some students with disabilities are also more likely to bully others. Therefore, parents must be alert to the signs of bullying and what they can do to intervene at home and to collaborate with school personnel.

Imagine how Derek's mother felt when she casually asked him if he was ever bullied on the school bus and he replied, "Always." His mother was shocked because he never mentioned it. She knew that he engaged in behaviors that others found off-putting, and he was not always socially appropriate. However, she knew the school recently instituted a bully-proof program, and there were no reports that he was ever bullied. When she pressed further and asked him how long this was going on, he said, "Forever." As she became more upset, she wanted to know why he never told her or his dad, why he never told anyone in school. His response floored her. Derek told her it was "a tradition." Sadly, he came to accept being a victim as a normal part of school, something that has always happened and probably always will. So why bother telling anyone? "They don't do anything anyhow" ended the discussion.

This is a sentiment shared by many students. As was reported in a previous chapter, teachers' perceptions of bullying and students' perceptions are markedly different. Anecdotal information suggests this is also true of differences in the perceptions of parents versus teachers. This, coupled with the fact that some students with disabilities may not comprehend the nature of bullying and are unsure or unable to report instances, makes it imperative that parents of students with disabilities are cognizant of this problem and know what to do. This chapter will provide parents with information that will enable them to protect their children from victimization. It will also provide parents whose children my engage in bullying behavior with ways to identify it and obtain the appropriate help.

Signs Your Child Might Be a Victim

There are a number of signs parents should look for at home as an indication that your child might be a victim:

- Missing belongings.
- Not eating lunch.
- Torn clothing.
- Unexplained bruises.
- Illness.
- Temper outbursts.
- School problems.
- Fear of going to school.
- Cutting classes.
- Isolation or staying in his or her room.
- Few or no friends.
- Never or infrequently being invited to parties.
- Avoiding school activities, especially lunch or recess.

The school nurse is an excellent source of information about the bully–victim problem. Children who are victimized in school make frequent visits to the school nurse. They may do this to avoid activities, especially during unstructured times of the day (lunch, recess, or dismissal), or they may go there because of illness or perceived illnesses. There is an association between victimization and common health problems in young children. Children who were being bullied reported not sleeping well, had headaches and stomachaches, felt sad, and wet their beds. Given this information, it would be wise to consult with the school nurse and not merely discuss the situation as a case of "trying to get out of things."

Parents need to be vigilant for these incidents of victimization. Being involved and interested in your child's school life is important. Being aware of your child's friends and activities will allow you to be more observant if a problem should arise. Ongoing, natural communication with your child will open up dialogue if bullying is occurring. This must go beyond merely asking "How was school today?" to an environment where children feel comfortable and reinforced for sharing their lives with their parents.

If you think there is a problem with bullies, you need to approach the school. You may be surprised to find out that they don't share your concern. This attitude is changing, but change takes time. Don't drop the issue. Pursue it through your parent–teacher association, school administration, or school board. The findings from anti-bullying programs in schools are very optimistic, but the first level is the recognition that the problem exists. And there is no denying it exists for students with disabilities.

What Should You Do?

In addition to making sure that the bullying prevention program is meeting the needs of your child (see Chapter 4), you can also provide them with positive experiences. They will begin to perceive themselves in ways other than being a victim.

- Know Your Child's Strengths and Weaknesses
  - Speak to your child's teacher to find out exactly what things your child does well and what areas are of concern. The teacher should provide you with his or her opinion about specific activities. It is not unreasonable to solicit advice on these concerns, but remember that it is advice, an opinion.

Thomas, a fourth-grade student with ADHD, was never interested in sports. Unfortunately, this made him a scapegoat in gym class and during recess. When he was picked to be on a team, he was always picked last. And his classmates continuously made fun of his lack of interest and ability. His math teacher shared the fact that Thomas loved statistics. The teacher talked to the physical education teacher (who was also the baseball coach) to see if he needed a statistician. Thomas began to work with the coach to perform a much-needed job. Students started seeing him as a valued member of the team and began to recognize his strengths.

- Select Activities That Focus on Strengths
  - You may think that by selecting activities in an area of weakness, you can encourage your child to improve certain skills. For example, you place your child, who has difficulty with fine motor control, in an origami program, thinking that the practice she gets will improve her fine motor control. On the contrary, the experience will probably be so negative that it will only reinforce her feelings of incompetence in this area. Activities outside of school should be enjoyable and positive and provide opportunities to succeed, not fail.
- Select Small Groups or Individualized Activities
  - Rather than having your child attend a large ice-skating class, try a few individual or small group lessons. The cost is not much different than a large class, and any initial success will give him the confidence he needs to continue to pursue the activity. Small groups and individualized activities reduce competition and comparisons. Your child will only have to do his best and not worry about how others are doing and how he stacks up against them.
- Encourage Special Interests and Hobbies
  - Few things excite children more than being an expert in a particular area. Having a special interest or hobby allows children to learn more about a subject than most children or adults. There are children who are experts on origami, rocks, gymnastics, snakes, race cars, baseball cards, and on and on. Adults have to ask *them* for information on these subjects. When these children show confidence in a special area of knowledge like this, their competence will spill over into their school lives, where the teacher can reinforce this interest.
  - Interests and hobbies don't just emerge. They are fostered by parents who give their children information through books, magazines, website links, and discussions and through taking them on trips to parks, zoos, museums, and other places of interest. A child who visited a Civil War battlefield became incredibly interested in the Civil War and started to listen to webcasts, view programs, and eventually read about it. He now knows more about it than most adults! He is proud to have a reputation for this in his school, where teachers sometimes seek him out with questions.
- Reinforce Effort
  - Sometimes children enjoy a particular activity, although they are not good at it. What do you do? Do you tell them not to join the soccer team because they are not well coordinated?

Or should they avoid the Cub Scouts because they become overwhelmed in large groups? One way to deal with the issue is to reinforce effort. Praise your child and his or her efforts, not necessarily the end result. They may never meet their or their parents' expectations, but they'll be more apt to succeed if their efforts are rewarded. Don't wait for him or her to reach some preconceived level of achievement—he or she may never reach it. But if you appreciate and praise small successes, he or she may achieve more than you'd expect.

- Ask Your Child What Activities He or She Wants to Participate In
  - This advice seems simple, but too often, we forget the obvious. Children will be more interested in participating in something they enjoy. Discuss any potential obstacles and how they can be overcome. More important, if it doesn't work out, allow your child to withdraw.

Parents also need to encourage and foster friendships with the vast majority of children who are not bullies. Some victims may not have the appropriate social skills necessary to develop friendships; therefore, this needs to be taught. Some children will have special educational needs that require more specific interventions for this skill. And others may lack the social perceptual skills (that is, understanding social situations) necessary to develop and maintain social relationships. These concerns need to be addressed, or else your child will fail and further reinforce his or her feelings of incompetence.

What to Do If Your Child Is a Bully

There are students with disabilities who bully others. Reasons cited in previous chapters focused on the lack of appropriate social skills and classroom environments. However, another component that parents must consider is their role in the process. It has been said that "bullies are made, not born."

Be a Good Role Model

Many parents have said that they never realized how careful they have to be in what they say and what they do because their kids will "throw it back" to them. Below are a few scenarios that discuss options available to parents and how each opinion might affect their child or children.

Scenario 1

You and your family are waiting in line in a department store, and someone bumps into you. Immediately, you tell that person to be careful and watch where she is walking. She apologizes, but you continue to speak in a harsh voice because you want to make your point that the person should be more careful. At this point, there are quite a few people staring at you, and the person walks away. You turn to your family, and with a satisfied look on your face, you say, "You have to let people know what you think."

Parents may think that this forceful approach to the outside world shows children that it is important to stick up for yourself. What it will likely teach children who are prone to bullying is that you need to constantly berate someone so that they will submit to you. It also shows children that every act should be perceived as provocation. And, finally, it demonstrates that creating a chaotic situation in a store full of people is something to be valued: "Who cares if people are looking—that's their problem" is an attitude that might be instilled.

An alternative to the above is to merely accept the apology and move on. It shows your children that people aren't perfect; sometimes people are inattentive, but it's not a big deal—be apologetic, and it's over. Even if she didn't apologize, you can simply ignore the behavior and perhaps tell your kids to be careful—sometimes people don't pay attention as they run through stores.

Scenario 2

You are out for a drive with your family, and a car cuts you off. You scream at the people inside, rush to pull up alongside of their car, start screaming at them, give them an obscene hand gesture, and drive off, mumbling what a bunch of jerks are on the road these days.

Some people will feel a sense of empowerment when they are in a car. In a well-publicized case in the New York City area, a couple, with an infant in the car, was cut off by another car and gave the driver an obscene gesture. The car caught up to them, and its driver shot and killed the woman and baby. This is clearly an extreme, but if you needed a reason to be passive in a car, then this is it.

Relatively calm people can become very aggressive when driving if they perceive a violation of the rules of the road. A mother of a three-year-old reported that her daughter corrected her when a car stopped abruptly in front of her. The mother yelled, "You stupid jerk," and the daughter said, "No, Mommy, you're supposed to say,

'You (expletive deleted) jerk.'" This child had learned that that was the typical response her mother made when this happened.

It's not wrong to get annoyed. What is clearly inappropriate is to try to resolve this issue through aggression on the road. Why not assume that the driver did not do this intentionally, beep your horn, and move on (literally)?

Scenario 3

Your child describes a scene at school where he characterizes one classmate as a "real dork" whom everyone makes fun of. He tells you how he looks so "out of it" in his peculiar clothes and has "weird" habits. You merely continue eating as he describes the rest of his day in school.

By ignoring these remarks, you are letting your child know that it's OK to make fun of someone, to ridicule the person, and to call him names. Kids will do this occasionally, but it is still important for parents to make a clear statement that it is not acceptable. Depending on your child's age, you might say, "It's really not nice to make fun of someone," or "It must be hard for this kid," or "I'm sure there is something you could like about him," or "Why don't you be nice to him, and maybe others will do the same," and the like. You need to let your children know at an early age that this is unacceptable behavior.

Scenario 4

You are in a restaurant when you overhear the conversation at the table next to you. The people are verbally abusive to the waitress, and you really don't know what the problem is, but it appears to be escalating, and the waitress appears to be overwhelmed.

If you choose to do nothing and act as if it never happened, you might be teaching your child to not get involved. Too much bullying occurs because the silent majority of children allow it to go on. Verbal interventions may not be appropriate because the bullies at the table will probably tell you to mind your own business. However, you can very matter-of-factly find the manager of the restaurant and let him or her know that the waitress needs assistance immediately. This serves as a model for your child to tell a teacher when he or she feels someone is being picked on and not merely to ignore it.

It's not easy being a role model, but you are one. You must recognize that, every time you interact with your children, you are teaching them something. As they observe the way you resolve conflicts both in and out of the home and family, they will begin to use these strategies with others. If these strategies are perceived as bullying, they will bully others to get their way.

Provide Social Skills Training

Many victims lack appropriate social skills. Parents can teach their child how to engage in these skills by working on them at home. Parents can also encourage their school district to provide specific social skills training and get it on the IEP. And in some cases, parents may seek out a professional who provides this type of training for groups of victims.

What are social skills? The ability to understand how your behavior affects others is a social skill; knowing how to make friends is a social skill; knowing when and where to say certain things is a social skill. Children who lack these skills may be unaware of the effect of their behavior on others, say the wrong thing at the wrong time, or have difficulty making friends.

A number of professionals have addressed this issue and have developed social skills training programs. These programs attempt to make children aware of their own behavior and to teach them how to act in socially appropriate ways (McNamara, 2007).

Most training programs have these five basic components:

1. Provide instruction.
2. Present a model.
3. Rehearse.
4. Provide feedback.
5. Practice.

Provide Instruction

Be as explicit as possible when describing the social skills you want to develop. Too often, children and adolescents know what they are not supposed to do but are vague when it comes to things they should be doing. Part of the reason for this behavior is lack of training. Social skills training forces us to identify exactly what the components of appropriate social behavior are and to describe them in a clear, unambiguous manner.

If you wanted to teach *walking assertively,* you would describe a few behaviors in which you could provide instructions. Here are some examples:

1. Walk with your head up.
2. Keep your shoulders back.
3. Look straight ahead.
4. Walk at a good pace.

Present a Model

A model is a demonstration of the desired behavior. At first, demonstrate what you want your child to do so that he or she can copy your behavior. Keep it simple. After you demonstrate the behavior, you should attempt to use different models. Some parents have been very successful with puppets, pictures, photographs, TV, videos, and books. Try to find anything that allows you to provide examples to your child of the social skill you are teaching. When selecting a model, make sure that the most important element clearly demonstrates the skill you are teaching.

In the example of walking assertively, parents can watch TV shows with their child and point out examples when the characters walk assertively. Parents can also show family videos and note those who are walking assertively. When reading with their children, parents can point out specific characters that are depicted walking in a self-assured manner.

If there are a lot of distracters, your child might focus on these and not on the skill you are teaching. Generally speaking, the more models you provide, the higher probability that learning will take place.

Rehearse

By rehearsing social skills, children are able to act out and practice the newly developed skill in a controlled environment. For many children, the most effective type of rehearsal is verbal and motor responding. Talk through each step of the skill, and allow your child to perform it. Role-playing can also be employed at this stage. However, role-playing has to be carefully orchestrated; otherwise, it will be a useless activity. It is more than you playing a role. You should clearly specify what behaviors your child is to perform and when he or she should perform them. Many children respond favorably to role-playing if it is carried out with this kind of specificity.

Parents can walk in a very passive way and play that role, while the child plays the assertive role. Other family members can carry out specific roles. For example, one child can role-play the bully and wait for the victim to walk past. And the child who is the victim can walk with his father in an assertive manner past the bully.

Provide Feedback

Without information about their performance, most children won't know how they did. This feedback is critical to the success of a social skills training program. Objective, nonevaluative feedback should be given for each task performed. Tell them what they did without criticism. Feedback can be corrective ("Try to walk a little taller") or reinforcing ("It's great the way you are looking straight ahead"). Some children benefit from video and audio feedback of their performance. They may perceive this as more objective than a parent giving feedback.

Parents can take their child to a mall and practice walking assertively. Try going to a local store or supermarket, and practice this skill. Attempt to practice in different settings, such as places where there are a lot of people or places where there are few, if any, people.

Another social skill that is often necessary for children who are victims is to establish eye contact with the bully. The five-step process is described below:

1. **Provide Instruction.** "When you speak to someone, look in his or her eyes. And when someone is speaking to you, look in that person's eyes."
2. **Present a Model.** There are endless examples of people using good eye contact in social settings. Parents can view movies, TV shows, and family videos; go to the beach, a restaurant, the mall, or any social setting, and there will be many models of this social skill.
3. **Rehearse.** Parents can role-play a child who is looking away from someone who is talking to them. Role-play at the dinner table, and alternate roles of good eye contact and poor eye contact. Don't comment negatively when your child is not using good eye contact. The purpose is to teach the appropriate skill, not to reprimand him or her when he or she doesn't demonstrate that skill.
4. **Provide Feedback.** Video the dinner interaction, and view it together. Let your child know when he or she engaged in the appropriate behavior and when he or she did not. Together, note what characterizes good eye contact from poor eye contact.

5. **Practice.** Finally, you are ready to go public. Reinforce all your child's attempts to use this skill. Every time he or she engages in proper eye contact, let him or her know how pleased you are with this new behavior.

The five-step procedure is extremely useful for parents. It provides a strategy for dealing with problematic behaviors in a reasonable manner. Children respond very positively because they are not being berated for their behavior but are being taught to engage in appropriate social skills. They also like it because they are receiving reinforcement at every step.

How to Deal With Cyberbullying

As previously noted, cyberbullying is a major concern for students with disabilities, and parents need to be aware of their child's online and social media activities. Typically, bullying prevention programs do not address cyberbullying directly, but 49 states have laws that protect victims. Moreover, most schools have a policy on cyberbullying, and you should request a copy from your district. AbilityPath (2012) suggests tips for parents so that they can protect their child with disabilities online (p. 50):

1. Teach your child to never reveal personal information online. Help children understand why it is important not to reveal details others should not "see."
2. Limit your child's online time. Set firm rules as to when and how long your child can be online. It's a good idea to allow your child to go online only when you're home to supervise these activities.
3. Through role-playing or social stories, teach your child what improper photos, videos, or threatening conduct might look like or feel like. If such instances occur, impress upon your child the immediate need not to respond to the messenger but instead to report it to you or another adult.
4. Keep copies of inappropriate messages, but as a parent, do not respond.
5. Do not dissuade your child from using technology such as cell phones for text messaging or Facebook for communication with peers. These tools are becoming increasingly a part of the way in which youth communicate, and to leave them out of such communication streams isolates them more. Instead,

teach them the proper use for the tools, and always insist that you become your child's friend on Facebook.

6. Research screening programs that allow you to "see" all the dialogue that your child has online.

7. Check text messages on cell phones frequently to make sure that derogatory messages are not being sent to your child.

8. Review the security settings on your computer or child's social networks. Be sure restrictions are placed on what information or images are viewed by friends as well as the public. Be sure your child can't access adult-only content or respond to scams in e-mail requests.

9. Check your child's Facebook page or other social networks, and observe their actions as well as their friends.'

10. Use resources such as www.safetyweb.com to know what information is available online about your child and the most recent news or resources available to protect them.

Use Your Child's Individualized Education Plan

Walk a Mile in Their Shoes (AbilityPath, 2011) provides excellent suggestions for using an IEP in the bullying prevention process (p. 27–29). (Also see www.pacer.org/bullying.) The specific examples they provide include the following:

- Improve social understanding by having goals focused around sharing, taking turns, or thinking before acting (PACER Center, 2003). Use concrete, real-world situations. The focus of this goal should not be to teach the child to be less teasable but should be interpersonal skill building.

- Participate in a social skills group. By being given the opportunity to practice social situations, role-playing, social stories, and other techniques with school peers, under adult supervision, the child may better identify and understand difficult situations when they occur. Groups such as this one can also facilitate friendships and a sense of not being alone.

- Increase self-advocacy skills. This way, the child can say "Stop that" or walk away.

- Help the child develop and learn a brief, nonconfrontational verbal response to the bully. Practice both direct and indirect ways to react to, handle, or avoid bullying behavior.

- Set speech and language goals. These goals should be set with the help of a speech and language specialist. They should focus on articulation, speech intelligibility, and language pragmatics.

- Increase the child's self-awareness about his or her disability. Learning their strengths and feeling proud of who they are and their accomplishments, while also understanding how their disability my impact them, particularly in social situations, is often important.
- Help the child identify bullying as well as how and to whom to report it. Keep in mind that some children may have a difficult time determining that they are targets of bullying behavior. Goals that help educate the child on the difference between reporting an incident and ratting or tattling as well as identifying the difference between playful teasing and hurtful teasing or bullying may be needed.
- Teach the child a signal system. This is for use when in need of friend or adult intervention.
- Identify and facilitate a relationship with a school staff person. This person can help the child make reports of incidents and provide the child with additional intervention and support.
- If social situations are impeding the child's ability to access their education, then they must be appropriately remedied. Being the target of bullying can bring some children's social needs into sharper focus. In addition to new goals, a new assessment may be appropriate.

Other supports, accommodations and strategies for the IEP team to consider are as follows:

- Monitor and supervise unstructured time. Increase hallway, bathroom, lunchroom, and playground monitoring by staff. Adult-monitored safe zones or having an adult shadow the child during these times is sometimes necessary.
- Educate the staff and other students about the child's assistive technology, 1:1 aide, interpreter, and other items that are different. Create a better understanding with staff of the child's disability and the necessary support that goes with it.
- Avoid certain situations or locations that can be "loaded" for a student.
- Keep the child away from the bully. Or keep the bully away from the child until things are resolved.
- Consider seating the student away from students who might tend to bully. Remember that being proactive can prevent incidents from occurring in the first place.

- Allow the child to leave class early. This can help to avoid hallway incidents.
- Take recess or lunch in a different setting. But still make sure some peers are present.
- Consider keeping the child from highly charged, competitive situations.
- Designate a peer buddy. Or have the classroom teacher foster a friendship between the child and a safe child. A classroom with cooperative learning activities is one mechanism to facilitate positive social interactions.
- Set up regular appointments with the school's psychologist. Or identify another safe person on the campus with whom your child can check in as an outlet, or allow for classroom breaks (either in or out of the classroom).

© AbilityPath.org, 2011, *Walk A Mile in Their Shoes: Bullying and the Child with Special Needs*

Using Section 504 of the Rehabilitation Act of 1973

Section 504 requires any institution that receives federal funds to make accommodations for individuals with disabilities. This is not a special education law but rather a civil rights law for all students. Disability is defined in broader terms than in IDEA as "any physical or mental impairment that substantially limits major life activities" (included are walking, talking, seeing, hearing, speaking, breathing, learning, working, performing manual tasks, setting, reaching, and staying). If the student has a disability under Section 504, the school is required to develop an accommodation plan. This can include extended time, a scribe, and a separate setting for tests. The Office of Civil Rights (OCR) Department of Education (1989, p. 8) provides a list of requirements for schools under Section 504 that protects the civil rights of individuals with disabilities. The school must do the following:

- Annually identify and locate all children with disabilities who are underserved.
- Provide a "free, appropriate public education" to each student with a disability, regardless of the nature or severity of the disability. This means providing general or special education and related aids and services designed to meet the individual educational needs of persons with disabilities as adequately as the needs of nondisabled persons are met.
- Ensure that each student with disabilities is educated with nondisabled students to the maximum extent appropriate.

- Establish nondiscriminatory evaluation and placement procedures to avoid the inappropriate education that may result from misclassification or misplacement of students.
- Establish procedural safeguards to enable parents and guardians to participate meaningfully in decisions regarding the evaluation and placement of their children.
- Afford children with disabilities an equal opportunity to participate in nonacademic and extracurricular services and activities.

Parents who have children with 504 plans can incorporate issues related to bullying in a similar manner that it is being utilized in the development and implementation of the IEP.

Best Practices for Parents

The Matrix Parents Network, as cited in *Walk a Mile in Their Shoes* (AbilityPath, 2011) lists the best practices for parents of students with disabilities regarding bullying (p. 15–17):

- Be aware that students often feel that adult intervention is infrequent and unhelpful and, as such, fear that telling adults will only bring more harassment from bullies.
- Be observant of a child's behavior, appearance, and moods, particularly if one thinks that a child is at risk for being bullied. If a child is reluctant to attend school, investigate why, and consider a negative social experience as one reason.
- If a parent suspects something is wrong, talk with the child. Children can be reluctant to speak up for fear of retaliation or because they don't want to tattletale. Whether it's a parent or the child who initiates the conversation, speak openly and honestly—and listen! Keep the conversation at a level a child can understand. Remember that every child is different; what may not bother one child might be extremely detrimental to another.
- Don't blame the child. Be supportive, loving, and patient. Take his or her story seriously. Let him or her know that it's not his or her fault and that appropriate action will be taken.
- Get details from the child about the incident(s). Try not to direct his or her responses, but ask pertinent questions about what happened and how he or she felt or feels. Let the child know that appropriate confidentiality will be kept, but that keeping bullying a secret is not good for anyone. Tell the child that he or she has the right to be safe.

- Stay focused on the child and the issue. Though a parent will likely be upset or angry for the child, overreacting (or under-reacting) can make things more stressful for a child. Allowing emotions to take over can also make an objective assessment of the situation more difficult. Keeping an emotional response in check will help one better support and advocate for the child.
- If appropriate, problem solve or brainstorm intervention strategies with the child. Giving him or her relevant information, such as the definition of bullying, at a level he or she can understand, can be helpful as well.
- Bullying should never be ignored. Intervene immediately. Children are easily emotionally wounded and often have few skills to cope. Follow up with the school as soon as possible. If needed, seek help from outside sources.
- Talk with pertinent school staff. Find out what they know and what actions, if any, they've taken. Make sure they understand the child's disability and the possible impact his or her disability might have on the social dynamics that set up bullying. The staff may not be aware of a problem, but once they are, work collaboratively on how best to help the child. Ongoing communication and the continued monitoring of resolved bullying issues are often necessary.
- Make sure that the staff speaks with the bully and victim separately. Depending on the age and needs of the child, a parent may want to be a part of the initial discussion that the staff has with the child.
- If needed, ask for a general or an IEP meeting to discuss the situation and solutions. Document the incidents in writing. Include the conversations with the child, staff, and so on.
- Record dates, who was involved, what was said, names of possible witnesses, the adverse effects on the child, and the school's responses and interventions. Stick to the facts.
- A written complaint to the district may be appropriate if the problem proves to be severe.
- Seek the help of outside professionals, such as a pediatrician or mental health provider. Depending upon the degree of the problem and your child's vulnerability, utilizing professional assistance sooner rather than later may be important.
- Consult with outside organizations. Violence prevention agencies can provide information on how to protect the child.

Organizations familiar with the child's disability and its unique characteristics may have some specific intervention ideas.

- If physical signs of the bullying exists (torn clothes, cuts, bruises, etc.), take a photo; police involvement may be needed.
- For the younger child, volunteering in his or her classroom might help one better understand the social dynamics and the underlying problems.
- Discuss the issue of bullying with other parents, individually or in a support group. Talking with the parents of the bully, or the bully him- or herself, is not recommended.
- Continue to assess and monitor the child. Is he or she physically and emotionally safe? If not, what further steps need to be taken? Provide ongoing opportunities for continued open discussions, checking in with the child regularly. If the child becomes more withdrawn, depressed, or reluctant to go to school or you see a decline in his or her academic performance, then take the issue back to the school. If the school does not use appropriate actions, then you may need to go higher up in the administration or take other actions, such as making a formal complaint.

© AbilityPath.org, 2011, *Walk A Mile in Their Shoes: Bullying and the Child with Special Needs*

When to Seek Professional Help

It is very difficult to change your own behavior. Parents have come to think that they should know exactly what to do and when to do it, and to do otherwise is to admit failure. Parents can learn effective parenting techniques in order to reduce the bullying behaviors of their children. They can change the behavior of their children.

There are times, however, when it's difficult to do it alone. You may need to seek the assistance of a professional. Knowing when to do so is critical. Below are a number of situations that will probably need the assistance of a professional.

- If you feel you can't control yourself and you want to hit your child. This is the number one reason why you should seek the help of a professional. Recently, a parent described an incident where she was riding the bus with her eight-year-old daughter who would not stop crying, and the mother said, "I thought that, if I just hit her head against the pole on the bus, she'd stop. I came very close to doing it." These feelings—that the only way to stop a behavior is to use physical (corporal) punishment—must be dealt with immediately. If you consider using force to stop a behavior, or if you frequently hit your child now, get help and get it soon. Call the child protective services agency in your area, or call the school, ask for the name of a professional who works with parents, and contact him or her immediately.

- If you see your child being physically abusive toward others. If your child is frequently observed hitting others and does not appear to be remorseful, seek help. Bullying occurs more frequently in school settings, so many parents say they've never observed their child bullying anybody. Therefore, if you see your child hitting others, biting others, and in general, inflicting harm when you have children over, at birthday parties, or at the playground, seek professional help—this is a serious problem.

- If your child is involved with the police. If your child has been involved in criminal behavior, such as robbing or beating up or threatening others, and has been arrested, this is clearly something serious, and help should be obtained as soon as possible. The bullying cycle starts early, but without intervention, there is an increased risk of criminal behavior.

- If you are frequently contacted by the school. If you receive a number of complaints from school officials that your child has been bullying other children, it is usually a real concern. A few instances are not a problem. But when a child is targeted by the school as a bully, parental intervention is critical. This is especially true if the school doesn't have a good anti-bully program, which is the next reason to seek professional help.

- You've tried some techniques, but they just didn't work. You have conscientiously tried to change your parenting techniques, but you have been unsuccessful. This happens to many parents. You need to relearn how to be an effective parent, and that takes time and effort. You may enroll in a parenting course but feel you need more specific, individualized assistance. You may try to carry out some of the procedures, like a contract or a token economy system, but it's just not working. There are many parents who truly try to change their own behavior but cannot do it without the assistance of a professional. And this is not long-term psychotherapy; this is goal-directed counseling or specific behavioral intervention that helps parents of bullies change their parenting styles. This, coupled with a school-based program, is very effective.

Summary

This chapter provided parents of students with disabilities with ways in which they can identify, intervene, and prevent bullying, either as a victim or a bully. Specific signs of victims and bullies were provided along with a number of things parents can do to decrease bullying or victimization. Parents were also provided with information on cyberbullying and using the IEP as a valuable tool in the bullying prevention process. Finally, parents were provided with information that will enable them to know when they need to seek professional help for their child.

TEST YOURSELF

1. What are the signs of victimization?
2. What are the signs of being a bully?
3. What can parents do to reduce the chances their child will be a bully or a victim?
4. How can parents protect their child from cyberbullying?
5. How can the IEP be utilized to provide services related to bullying?
6. When should parents seek professional services?

8

Teaching Supports and Techniques

This chapter will focus on instructional approaches and strategies that meet the needs of students with disabilities in programs that address bullying. These should not be viewed as additional work or activities that supplement a school-wide program and will be a burden for teachers of students with disabilities. Rather, they should be viewed as an integral part of good teaching. You are probably utilizing them in academic and behavioral interventions. They are presented here as a way to fortify the anti-bullying program for those students who are most at risk for being victims. If a school-wide program is truly school wide and addresses all learners, teachers of students with disabilities must employ best practices when providing instruction on bullying as they do with the acquisition of basic skills and content area subjects. This chapter will discuss ways in which positive behavioral support (PBS) programs, collaborative teaching, and differentiated instruction can be applied to a bullying prevention program as well as to create a kind and caring classroom. Finally, it will discuss ways to infuse social skills into the curriculum.

Utilize the Existing Positive Behavioral Supports

The reauthorization of IDEA in 2004 required schools to provide "positive behavioral supports to ensure that every student with a disability receives a free appropriate public education." PBS has been employed from the primary grades through high school and in school-wide programs (McNamara, 2007). Ross and Horner (2009) and Good, McIntosh, and Geitz (2011) discuss ways in which schools can integrate bully-prevention programs into the existing PBS. They note that this may be the most beneficial to students with disabilities because they are most likely to be bullied. The data provided by Good and colleagues (2011) show promising results, with the added appeal of merely integrating the practices into a program that was already in place. The four major components of PBS (OSEP Technical Assistance Center on Positive Behavioral Interventions and Supports, 2003, p. 2), as stated in McNamara (2007), include the following:

1. **Behavioral Expectations Are Defined.** A small number of clearly defined behavioral expectations are defined in positive, simple rules, for example:
   - Be respectful, be responsible, and be safe.
   - Respect yourself, respect others, and respect property.

2. **Behavioral Expectations Are Taught.** The behavioral expectations are taught to all students in the building and are taught in real contexts. The goals of the teaching are to take broad expectations (like be respectful) and provide specific behavioral examples. (In class, being respectful means raising your hand when you want to speak or get help. During lunch or in the hall, being respectful means using a person's name when you talk to him or her.) Teaching appropriate behavior involves much more than simply telling students what behaviors they should avoid. Behavioral expectations are taught using the same teaching norms applied to other curricula. The general rule is presented, the rationale for the rule is discussed, positive examples (the right way) are described and rehearsed, and negative examples (the wrong way) are described and modeled. Students are given an opportunity to practice the right way until they demonstrate fluent performance.

3. **Appropriate Behaviors Are Acknowledged.** Once appropriate behaviors have been defined and taught, they need to be acknowledged on a regular basis. Some schools do this through formal systems (tickets or rewards); others do it through social events. Schools that are successful in creating a competent culture typically establish a pattern in which adult interactions with students are positive four times as often as they are negative. To achieve this standard, some strategy is

needed to build and maintain positive adult initiations with students (both in class and outside of class).

4. **Behavioral Errors Are Corrected Proactively.** When students violate behavioral expectations, clear procedures are needed for providing information to them that their behavior was unacceptable and preventing that unacceptable behavior from resulting in inadvertent rewards. Students, teachers, and administrators all should be able to predict what will occur when behavior errors are identified.

Bully Prevention in Positive Behavioral Support (BP-PBS) is an excellent example of the integration of a bullying prevention program into an existing PBS program. It focuses on decreasing bullying and teaches victims, and potential victims, appropriate responses.

The BP-PBS program provides a training manual for both elementary and middle school and is also available in French and Spanish (www.pbis.org). Ross, Horner, and Stiller (2011) present six key features of their program:

1. The use of empirically based principles.
2. Monitoring and acknowledgement of students for appropriate behavior.
3. Specific instruction to prevent bullying behavior from being rewarded by others.
4. Use of a consistently administered continuum of consequences.
5. Use of data to evaluate and guide decision making.
6. Establishment of a collaborative team to develop, implement, and manage the program.

The last key feature provides an excellent opportunity for the involvement of teachers of students with disabilities, given the high probability that these students will be victims or may engage in bullying. The model also affords the opportunity to provide services in a proactive, rather than reactive, manner. The program utilizes the three-tier model advocated by Walker, Horner, Sugai, Bullis, Sprage, and colleagues (1996). The primary tier would be employed for all students, the secondary tier for those students who are at risk, and the tertiary tier for students who are at high risk for bullying. At the very least, students with disabilities should be targeted for Tier 2, if not Tier 3, interventions. School-wide programs have not been effective for these students for the reasons described throughout this book. Therefore, a more focused approach, including modifying assessments and curriculum materials and providing differentiated instruction must be implemented. For example, when using the stop, walk, and talk response to bullying as presented in BP-PBS (see pbis.org for the entire program), there are modifications that students with disabilities may need in order to be able to carry out these responses. When presenting the stop signal, it is recommended that teachers present three correct examples of when to use the stop signal and one or two examples of when not to use it.

The examples you provide should be concrete and utilize the real-life experiences that you've observed your students encountering in school. You will probably need to provide more examples than are recommended. You can also simplify the language or provide pictures or videos with examples of students using the stop signal. More frequent practice and reinforcement will also be necessary. Some students with intellectual disabilities and students on the autism spectrum may not realize when they are being bullied or when they might be perceived as a bully. Additional time, lower-level materials, and a variety of presentations may need to be employed. For some students, you may need to divide the lesson into smaller components and spread it over time because they may not be able to attend, stay on task, or sustain attention. This will be particularly true for students with ADHD but may also be necessary for other students who have difficulty with attention.

Step 2 is walk away, and the authors of BP-PBS recommend modeling the walk away response when the stop signal is ineffective. Again, three positive examples of when to use the walk away response are suggested and one example of when not to use it. This is a particularly difficult concept for students because they have to recognize when the stop signal is ineffective. Too often, students employ the same strategy or technique even though it has not reduced the bullying. Therefore, you will need to provide extensive examples of specific situations when it did not work. As students share their experiences and as you collect data from other staff members, you will be better able to assess if they are carrying out the stop signal correctly and it is not working or if they are not implementing it correctly. If the student has a one-to-one paraprofessional, he or she will be able to provide you with information (and data) on how effective the strategy is for the student and allow you to provide additional instruction. When providing examples of when it is appropriate to walk away, you should include examples of the stop signal and ask students to decide which is the best strategy to employ. They can do this in small groups or pairs and then share their thoughts with the whole group. Once you feel they know the stop response, you can move on to walk away. As you model this response, start with simple, concrete, easily observable examples before you move on to more subtle and not-so-obvious examples of bullying. Students with social perceptual difficulties and those lacking social skills (which may include a number of disabilities) will need a great deal of instruction on those incidents that are not so clearly bullying but could lead to bullying.

The last step is to talk; that is, tell an adult. Knowing when to tell an adult is difficult for any student because they may think that it is tattling. The BP-PBS program suggests discussing the difference between talking (telling on someone just to get them in trouble) and telling an adult in order to stop the bullying. All students need to know that they can talk to any adult in the school about bullying and it will never get back to the bully. Again, you will need to modify the presentation with numerous examples of when it is appropriate to tell and reinforcement for doing so. Despite this, there will probably be students who will use the tell response as the first step. And while that is not the ultimate goal of the program, it is important to recognize that bullying is serious and harmful and adults should intervene. If the adult's response is "Work it out yourself, then see me," many students will simply suffer in silence rather than seek help when it is not forthcoming. See Raskauskas and Modell (2011) for an excellent case study of the implementation of BP-PBS into existing PBS.

Utilize a Collaborative Teaching Model

Students with disabilities are frequently placed in collaborative classes with two certified teachers: one special educator and one general educator (McNamara, 2007; Friend & Cook, 2013). This classroom placement provides students with disabilities appropriate models for classroom behavior, both academic and social. It provides the general education student with an awareness of the diverse needs of their classmates. As previously noted, students with disabilities who were placed in this model were less likely to be bullied or to be a bully. It was also noted that, for this to be effective as a protective factor in bullying, it must be carried out correctly. This section of the chapter will describe the major components of a collaborative model and factors that can lead to success.

Friend and Cook (2013) and others (McLeshey & Waldron, 2002; Wiess & Lloyd, 2002) cite the defining characteristics of collaboration:

- Collaboration is voluntary.
- Collaboration requires parity among participants.

- Collaboration is based on mutual goals.
- Collaboration depends on shared responsibility for participation in decision making.
- Individuals who collaborate share resources.
- Individuals who collaborate share accountability for actions.

Unless these defining characteristics are addressed, the coteaching teams will not function as effectively as they could. Clearly, there are times when all of these cannot be addressed, for example, voluntary membership. However, the goal is to move in the direction of addressing all of the characteristics and modify or adapt them depending upon your school's needs. More specific information on each characteristic is provided below.

Collaboration Is Voluntary

Collaboration works best when school personnel participate in the collaboration process. They view this as valuable and believe that, if they share ideas, expertise, and beliefs, students will benefit. They enjoy working on teams, like to share ideas, and thrive on interpersonal contact. And yet, in many small school districts, it is difficult to carry out state and federal mandates, such as developing prereferral teams, solely on a volunteer basis. There are teachers and support staff who should be on the team or coteach. Therefore, waiting for volunteers may not be the best approach. Certain "volunteers" may need to be selected—those who everyone agrees are critical for the success of the team. This does not suggest that the process should be closed; it merely recognizes that, in small school districts, volunteers may need to be encouraged. Some school districts provide incentives for volunteers, such as credits, training, or extra pay. In certain school districts, most frequently, coteachers are not volunteers but rather nontenured personnel. Too often, teams are overloaded with nontenured staff members who feel (rightly or wrongly) that they cannot refuse to collaborate if they want to receive tenure. Most teachers recognize that collaboration is here to stay and appreciate its benefits, but they may have too many other professional responsibilities. Therefore, while voluntary collaboration is a goal, it may not always be possible.

Collaboration Requires Parity Among Participants

Effective collaborative teams value the input of all members. Good coteachers value each other's expertise. Without parity, it is difficult to function as a team. Parity does not mean that everyone has the same competencies. It merely means that all team members participate, and their expertise and opinions are valued. No one member has more power than another. Obviously, schools are hierarchical. The principal is in charge. There are veteran teachers with seniority and new, nontenured teachers. Yet, for a collaborative team to function, all members must see each other as equal. The principal is just one member of the team when they are discussing options for a student.

If the principal overrides team decisions or does not allow adequate input from all members, the team will not be able to function effectively. With certain administrative structures and personalities, this may be a serious impediment.

Collaboration Is Based on Mutual Goals

This does not suggest that team members will always share the same goals. It does mean that they are clear on the goal of the team. How that goal will be reached will vary, but the mission should be clear. For example, all members of the prereferral team are to ensure that everything has been done for a student prior to a referral. Some members may view the team as a stalling tactic, postponing the inevitable classification. Others may view it as another mandate that will hurt their students and keep the numbers down. And still others may view it is a worthwhile process. A team with these members will not be able to function because their goals are so disparate. There may be disagreement on the specifics of the prereferral plan, but if the overall goal of the team is not mutually agreed upon, collaboration will not be possible.

Collaboration Depends on Shared Responsibility for Participation in Decision Making

Shared responsibility does not mean equal responsibility. In coteaching teams on the secondary school level, the content area specialist may do most of the content area instruction. The special education teacher may be responsible for identifying those students who are not grasping the content and providing alternative approaches. This may not always work out to an equal division of labor, yet it is shared. The prereferral team may decide that a behavior plan needs to be developed for a particular student. Not every member of the team can do this, but all can participate on some level and share in the decision-making process. Over time, if roles appear to be dramatically unequal, teams need to reevaluate the way members participate, deliberate, and make decisions.

Individuals Who Collaborate Share Resources

For collaboration to succeed, all parties must share their resources. Therefore, if the speech pathologist has materials appropriate for a third grader who is being discussed by the prereferral team, they should be shared. If a social studies teacher has workbooks that are helpful in preparing for state assessments, then these should be shared. Fortunately, most school personnel are more than willing to share their ideas and resources. If they are not, they are not good candidates for a collaborative project.

Individuals Who Collaborate Share Accountability for Actions

Sometime in your school career, you have worked on a group project and felt that you did most of the work and that others were not responsible. This can happen in collaborative arrangements.

A coteacher says that he will call a parent and forgets to do so. A meeting is scheduled for 9 a.m., and someone forgets to reserve the room. It is up to the other members to function as a team and assume the responsibilities of the weak member. Hopefully, over time, responsibilities will balance out. If not, it will be necessary to reconsider the composition of the team.

Certain characteristics emerge over time. Initially, it may be difficult to get staff members to participate. Over time, they begin to trust one another, enjoy working together, and develop a sense of community. Finally, the collaboration reaches a point where other staff members become interested. When they see the benefits of collaboration and the increased satisfaction of their colleagues, they want to be included.

Coteaching Models

There is consensus among professionals regarding coteaching models (see Friend & Cook, 2013, for additional information). There are six models:

One Teach, One Observe

In this arrangement, one teacher is responsible for providing instruction, while the coteacher observes a particular student or group of students for specific reasons. For example, a math class in a middle school utilized this approach because the teachers could not figure out where a particular student broke down in writing specific equations. This method can also be utilized when there is a question about note-taking skills or attending behaviors.

One Teach, One Drift

One teacher circulates around the classroom assisting students, checking work, making sure they understand the lesson, and so on. The coteacher is responsible for the overall lesson. In a kindergarten class, one teacher might explain how to make a mask using a variety of materials, while her coteacher moves about the room to make sure that all students are following the directions.

Station Teacher

Typically, the class is divided into three or four work stations. The students move from station to station and complete each task. If there are three stations and two teachers, one station may call for independent work. In a middle school English class on poetry, one group utilized the computer to research a poet, another group read poems from various poets, and still another group wrote their own poems. In a high school English class, the students were assigned to five groups. Each group went to a station where members had to respond to specific questions about a book they were reading. They wrote their responses using a colored marker and evaluated the responses of other groups. At 10-minute intervals, they moved to another station. Both teachers moved to various stations to comment on the work, respond to questions, and reinforce the group's effort and behavior.

Parallel Teaching

The coteacher divides the class in half, and each teacher teaches the same lesson. This reduces the class size and enables the teachers to assess students throughout the lesson. It also provides more opportunities for individual attention and reinforcement. It can be used in math classes, where complex problems with multiple directions are introduced. By dividing the class, the teachers can identify problems and use various methods to meet the needs of the smaller groups.

Alternate Teaching

This arrangement allows one teacher to provide different instructions to a smaller group. It is useful when teachers need to reinforce a previous lesson, teach prerequisite skills, or provide for practice.

If the teacher realizes that all the students who need these interventions have learning disabilities, the grouping strategies should be reconsidered.

Team Teaching

In this free-flowing approach, both teachers are responsible for instruction at the same time. They may alternate parts of the lesson, but neither one has the primary role. One may move around the room and interject a comment about a particular procedure. The two teachers mesh together, function as one, and begin to complete each other's sentences. When team teaching works well, there is a chemistry that makes learning exciting. However, there are potential problems when both teachers feel compelled to teach. There may simply be too much adult talk, and many students may find it distracting and difficult to focus on what is relevant and what is not.

How Do You Decide Which Coteaching Approach to Use?

A lot depends on the personalities and teaching styles of the coteachers. However, it seems reasonable to try different approaches, depending upon the grade and subject taught. Trying different approaches also avoids the problems of getting into a rut and using the same approach repeatedly. In addition, it helps to ensure parity as each coteacher is seen in a variety of roles.

Not every approach is applicable to every collaborative classroom. Teachers tend to develop a preference for one or a few approaches. However, the goal is to utilize both professionals to the maximum extent possible and model kind and caring behaviors in their classroom. The different competences of each teacher will enable them to meet the needs of all students. Below are examples of ways in which you can use each model when you are presenting a lesson on bullying from your school-wide program, specifically a lesson on What Is Bullying?

One Teach, One Observe/One Teach, One Drift

As one teacher discusses the concept of bullying, as described in your school-wide program, the other teacher can circulate the room to reinforce on-task behavior, note if students are having difficulty with the lesson, and provide clarification. This teacher may observe that the reading materials are too difficult or the lesson too long, or that the students cannot sustain attention. This can be useful information in planning subsequent lessons as well as addressing these concerns immediately during the lesson.

Stations

One station can have written material on bullying on a level commensurate with the students' reading ability. It can also have a video or audio presentation (iPad, MP3 player, etc.) for those students who may have difficulty reading. This will be the independent station. The two remaining stations will be teacher directed. One station can have scenarios of students who are bullying and those who are not, and they can identify the correct scenario. This can also be presented orally by the teacher, or have students read a few scenarios on their own, or use video or audio presentations. The last station can have students role-playing bullying and non-bullying scenarios (with specific role-playing instruction) and decide which ones are examples of bullying and which ones are not. They rotate the stations every 15 minutes.

Parallel

The major purpose of parallel teaching is to reduce the number of students you are teaching. Simply divide the students into two heterogeneous groups, and present the lesson on bullying. You can vary the lesson between groups, but typically it is the same. You may decide that some students prefer information presented visually and others auditorily, and you can divide them based on these preferences. You should use all of the effective teaching practices you typically use; only now, you have the advantage of having a small group, it will be easier to keep them focused, and you can assess their performance more rapidly. This will allow you to adjust your instruction.

Alternative

You know, based on previous data and experience, that some students will have difficulty with the concept of bullying. You can work with these students in a small group and provide information on a lower level, making modifications to the presentation. The remainder of the class is engaged in a typical lesson. Another example of how you can use alternative teaching in the bullying prevention program is when you know that the vocabulary will be too difficult for some of your students. These students can work in a small group, with more drills and practice, while the rest of the class is going over some general information related to bullying. When you feel they have mastered the vocabulary, they can join the rest of the class.

There are times after the lesson is completed that some students need additional reinforcement of the concept of bullying. One teacher can ask students if they need additional help or want to go over something from the previous lesson; he can ask them to join him at the small table. Any student can join him, and his coteacher can assist students as they practice what they were taught.

Coteachers need to be provided with time to plan their lessons and develop a collaborative relationship. They should be provided with ongoing staff development and an opportunity to share their experiences regarding the coteaching models they find most effective when modifying the school-wide bullying prevention program.

Creating an Empathetic Classroom

Not all students are placed in collaborative classrooms. However, that does not mean that there is no way to have a positive classroom environment. The Special Olympics (n.d., www.specialolympics.org) refers to themselves as a "global social movement." They provide wonderful opportunities for individuals with intellectual and developmental disabilities (IDD). They raise awareness and break stereotypes. Many school districts provide support and volunteers to assist with the games and other events. A mere perusal of the stories of these athletes is inspiring and can serve as a way to change attitudes toward individuals with disabilities and reduce bullying. One of their programs Best Buddies (n.d., www.bestbuddies.org) pairs students in middle school and high school with students with IDDs in order to establish and maintain one-to-one friendships. For those students who are placed in more restrictive environments, this is a powerful way to provide positive interactions and create a culture of caring. Other schools have friendship clubs that have similar goals or leadership clubs that encourage volunteering. The appeal of Best Buddies is that there is a great deal of support available to schools, and it is an ongoing relationship that is positive and genuine.

Most statewide initiatives that aim to reduce bullying also recognize that it is crucial to emphasize social and emotional learning. For example, New York's DASA addresses harassment and bullying but also states that it addresses the following:

- Interpersonal relationships.
- Respect for diversity.

- Emotional well-being and sense of safety.
- Student engagement.
- School, family, and community collaboration.

Some things that all teachers can do, regardless of the classroom placement, are listed below:

- Write a positive comment about every student in the class.
- Keep a kindness journal (students should also do this).
- Ask students, "Who has done something kind and caring for you?"
- Display a kind words list in your classroom.
- Model kind and caring behaviors.
- Treat students with respect.
- Use high rates of praise.
- Make a list of the things that people who are kind do.
- Do not use sarcasm.
- Use high rates of nonverbal approval (smiles, high fives, etc.).
- Keep track of acts of kindness and caring in your class.
- Reward acts of kindness and caring.
- Teach specific social skills.

I recall being in a classroom where a child sneezed. The teacher very matter-of-factly gave her a tissue. Without missing a beat, a classmate got up, went to an easel with a chart properly labeled "Acts of Kindness and Caring," wrote, "Ms. James gave Kerri a tissue," and sat down and joined her classmates. There must have been 300 acts on that list! The teacher told me she started this a few months ago and already noticed an increase in empathetic behavior. When they reach a certain amount, they will have a celebration. They want to put all of them in a book and share the list with their families and the entire school.

A Look Inside a Well-Managed Kind, Caring, and Respectful Classroom

As you walk into Mr. Bernes's classroom, one thing is obvious: Everyone is on task and working cooperatively. He has posters hanging on the wall with words of encouragement. There are pictures of students engaged in kind and caring behaviors. On one wall is a Kind Words Wall, and students are placing new words on it throughout the day. Next to the wall is an easel with a chart properly listing all the acts of kindness and caring his class (including him) have engaged in.

There are books all over, organized by level, genre, and interest. One section includes a large number of books on bullying.

The classroom rules are clearly stated and visible for all to see:

- We will be kind and caring and respectful.
- We will not bully.
- We will include everyone.

As Mr. Bernes moves around the room, he is smiling and praising all those students who are working and completing tasks. He pays particular attention to those who are kind to each other, help out each other, explain things to their classmates, and make the class a positive learning environment. He "catches them when they're good" and rarely has to reprimand. Sporadically, he gives students tickets that say "I was caught caring" on them. Initially, he gave them every time the behavior occurred but began delivering them intermittently when it was clear the behavior was happening frequently. Every day, he has a lottery. He places all the tickets in a jar and pulls three out, and those students can select from a list of rewards they decided on at the beginning of the month. These are little things, like a homework pass or being first in line or delivering things to the office. If the class gets a specified, agreed-upon number for the month, they have a kindness party to celebrate and share their acts of kindness and caring. They also invite a paraprofessional who they think is kind and caring.

The class has a monthly newsletter that keeps their families informed about just about everything they are doing, with a specific section for acts of kindness and caring. He sends home notes to parents sporadically informing them of how kind and caring their child was on that day. And he encourages parents to share the acts of kindness and caring their families are engaged in outside of school and to share these with the class.

As often as he can, Mr. Bernes will discuss a current event about bullying that he saw in the paper or on the Internet. He wants students to be aware of what is going on and ways they can solve some issues if they arise in his class. Hardly a day goes by without a bully incident in the news, and most recently, they appear to be overwhelmingly related to cyberbullying. He wants his students and their families to know what this is, how it takes place, and what to do about it.

While this might seem overwhelming at first, and you may wonder how he gets anything else accomplished, it is simply a matter of focus. It is a well-run classroom, where the reinforcement for display-ing kind, caring, and respectful behavior makes it an environment where students can flourish. They are on task, productive, and appre-ciate each other.

Differentiate Instruction

Differentiate instruction (DI) principles and practices are perfectly suited to meeting the needs of students with disabilities in any anti-bullying program. One feature of DI that makes it particularly appealing to bully prevention is the emphasis on a positive classroom environment as a critical component for learning. "Building a com-munity of learners who care for and support one another is essential in a differentiated classroom. Students who know and respect each other are more tolerant of differences and more comfortable when tasks are different" (Chapman & Gregory, 2007, p. 18). This chapter will present basic components of DI, followed by the application to a bully prevention program.

Basic Components

Teachers should differentiate instruction based on the readiness level, the interest level, or the learning profile of each student. They differentiate the content, the process, the products, and the learning environment (Tomilson, 1999; Bender, 2007).

- Content is what the student needs to learn.
- Process refers to the activities utilized to teach the content.
- Products are how students demonstrate what they have learned.
- Learning environment is the classroom climate.

Teachers will vary these components in order to meet the needs of all learners in their classrooms. The following examples are based on the work of a number of authors (Tomilson, 1999; Chapman & Gregory, 2007; Bender, 2007; Salend, 2008; Mercer, Mercer, & Pullen, 2012) and examples gathered from classroom teachers who use DI.

Content
- Vary reading materials.
- Use videos.
- Try listening centers.

- Employ small group instruction.
- Give students choices.
- Use a variety of technology.

Process

- Provide for different levels of instruction, referred to as *tiered lessons.*
- Develop centers based on student interest.
- Allow students to help each other.
- Utilize class-wide peer tutoring.
- Provide multiple levels of support.
- Use graphic organizers.
- Solicit student input on presentation of information.
- Make groups flexible.
- Be flexible in times for completion.
- Utilize learning contracts for groups or individuals.
- Be specific about expectations for learners.

Products

- Provide a variety of options for demonstrating understanding.
- Teach students to assess their products.
- Teach self-monitoring.
- Provide a variety of grouping options.
- Have clear, explicit, measurable expectations.
- Use rubrics.

Learning Environment

- Provide distraction-free options in the classroom.
- Allow for various work options; that is, sitting on carpet squares, at desks, standing, and so on.
- Use culturally diverse and sensitive materials.
- Establish classroom routines.
- Establish classroom rules.
- Reinforce appreciation of the needs of others.

As you differentiate the content, process, products, and learning environment, you can assess the student in order to see if he or she has the necessary skills for the lesson (readiness), has specific interests that can be tapped to engage him or her more fully in the lesson (interests), and has a specific way the student learns best (learning profile). This can be overwhelming at first, and all of the professional literature on DI suggests that you go slowly at first and not attempt to do all of the above at once. However, it should be apparent that many special education teachers do many of these every day, whether or not they call it DI. The task here is to apply DI to an area of relative neglect, that is, an area of social-emotional learning and specifically bully prevention. The following section will discuss a variety of DI procedures and techniques that are useful in this regard.

Differentiating Instruction and Bully Prevention

DI in the school-wide bully prevention program will allow you to meet the needs of students with a wide range of disabilities. The ongoing assessment and the variety of opportunities for students to learn and demonstrate competence are consistent with the basic precepts of special education instruction.

Know Your Students!

You must know as much as possible about your students prior to instruction in the bully prevention program. Special education teachers have a wealth of information, including reports from psychologists, social workers, education evaluators, and perhaps developmental pediatricians, psychiatrists, or neurologists. You will also have the IEP, previous teachers' records, and parental input. This allows you to gather information on the student's readiness, interests, and learning profile. When providing training in the school-wide program, the interests of the student may not be as relevant as in other areas of the curriculum, but it still should be considered. The strengths, weaknesses, academic performance, and basic skill levels will allow you to hypothesize as to the most appropriate level of material and the complexity of the tests you present. The information you gather for the learning profile will allow you to plan to use a variety of modalities (auditory, visual, tactile, or kinesthetic) and decide which are the most effective ways your students acquire knowledge. It is also important to pretest their knowledge regarding bullying. Their prior knowledge base may vary, and they may have many misconceptions. A simple way to assess this and to engage them in the lesson with a KWL graphic organizer. An example of how it can be utilized when you modify the school-wide program is provided in Figure 8.1.

Figure 8.1   KWL Graphic Organizer for Bullying

K What I Know	W What I Want to Know	L What I Learned
It's bad	Why do they do it?	
It's wrong	Why doesn't anybody stop them?	
They are mean	What should I do?	
Happens to me all the time	What can I say?	
No one stops them	Not sure	
It happens at lunchtime	Why do they always pick on special education students?	
They do it on the bus	Why can't the driver report them?	

The teacher began the lesson with a KWL chart on the SMART Board. One teacher led the discussion, and the coteacher wrote the responses. He asked them, "What do you know about bullying?" Once they came up with a reasonable number of responses, he moved on to the next section of the chart, the W. "What do you want to know about bullying?" Once again, as the teacher solicited responses, the other wrote them on the board. The last column, L, will remain empty until the end of the lesson when he will ask the class, "What have we learned about bullying?" The information from the last section is just one way in which the teacher can assess what the students learned.

Differentiate the Content

The ways in which you can differentiate content is obvious for some students with disabilities. For example, a student who is Deaf will most likely require a sign language interpreter, and for those students who are blind, you can choose from a variety of text readers, Braille, or other devices that your particular student finds effective (consult a professional in your district who is competent in teaching students who are Deaf or students who are visually impaired). However, for most students, it will require ongoing assessment and frequent consultation with colleagues who work with your students, such as the speech and language pathologist or behavioral consultant. The information you glean from this and the student's records and IEP will help you provide appropriate instruction. Some ways to differentiate the content of the bullying prevention program include the following:

- Provide listening centers with vignettes of bullying.
- Use videos of bullying (see www.stopbullying.gov).
- Role-play scenarios of bullying prevention.
- Provide a range of books on bullying.
- Use tablets for selecting from a range of e-books on bullying.
- Have students who have more knowledge about bullying (see KWL chart) teach other students.
- Utilize coteaching models.

More schools are making technology more accessible to students so that the method of presentation is easier to vary. Some districts provide iPads, NOOKs, and other tablets for students. This allows for easy access to reading material for immediate use in your classroom. Students can use devices, such as an MP3 player, iTunes, and others to provide auditory input. The more you differentiate the content, the more likely you will address a variety of needs, regardless of the specific special education classification.

Differentiate Products

There are many ways that students can demonstrate competence. How will you know what they've learned? Based on their needs, you can allow them to show you what they've learned in a number of ways. The following are some products that are appropriate for bullying prevention. Collaborate with your colleagues, solicit student input, and you will be able to generate many more.

- Write a bullying scenario.
- Role-play a bullying scenario.
- Make an anti-bullying poster.
- Make an anti-bullying video.

- List the signs of bullying.
- Discuss with a classmate ways to reduce bullying.
- Interview a teacher about bullying.
- Interview your parent or family member about bullying.
- Compile a list of books on bullying that are appropriate for your class.
- Make a PowerPoint presentation on what to do if you are bullied.
- Make up a test on bullying.
- Make a list of what you should do if you see someone being bullied.
- Interview students who were bullied.
- Develop a flowchart on what you should do if you are being bullied.
- Start an advice column on bullying in your school paper or for your class.

Anchoring Activities

What do you do when students are finished with an activity before others? In a truly differentiated classroom, this will surely happen. These activities, referred to as *anchoring activities,* are not busy work. They should be meaningful, engaging, and related to bullying. You can have a file or box or folder in the room identified as "Anchoring," and students can select from a variety of activities. Many are similar to differentiated products. Some possible activities include the following:

- Provide pictures of various bullying incidents, and have students provide captions.
- Provide questions students have to respond to, such as, "How would you feel if someone called you a bully?" or "Should you tell on a bully if he or she is your best friend?"
- Provide books, audio presentations, videos, and games to expand their knowledge.
- Students can make up a board game based on bullying.
- List incidents and non-incidents of bullying, and have students select which ones are examples of bullying.
- Provide data on bullying in your school, and have students analyze it and provide remedies.

In addition to reinforcing and expanding learning, it also highlights the importance of dealing with bullying as an ongoing process, not merely a few lessons.

Figure 8.2 provides you with a checklist that enables you to assess your progress in DI in your classroom.

Figure 8.2   Differentiating Instruction Checklist

Have You . . .

1. Pretested your students?
2. Gathered all the relevant information from their files, including the IEPs?
3. Provided a variety of reading material on different levels?
4. Provided listening centers in the classroom?
5. Allowed for movement in your classroom?
6. Involved students as peer tutors?
7. Provided a number of ways to demonstrate competence?
8. Provided anchoring activities?
9. Created a kind and caring learning environment?
10. Collaborated with colleagues on differentiated practices?

Include Social Skills and Bullying Prevention Into the Curriculum

There is no doubt that time is a valuable commodity in most classrooms throughout the United States. There are teachers who feel they have no time in their day to provide instruction on bullying prevention with all the other subjects they must teach. One way to deal with these real-time constraints is to utilize the content of your curriculum to introduce issues related to bullying.

During a presentation in a third-grade class, a student asked if the book they were reading, *The Hundred Dresses,* was an example of bullying. It was. It is a story of a poor girl, Wanda, who is teased about her name and her clothes. She wore the same dress every day. Wanda claimed to have 100 dresses. The girls in her class teased her so much about this "lie" that the family moved. I won't tell you how it ends, except that it addresses bullying, remorse, and character development. The teacher did not recognize the relationship to the topic of discussion, but the students did. Many teachers infuse character education and kindness throughout their content areas. One particularly good website, from Bellemore-Merrick UFSD (n.d.) is www.bellmore-merrick.k12.ny.us (search for DASA). In response to New York State's DASA, the site provides examples of how bullying, harassment, and discrimination can be infused into their Grade 7 through 12 curriculums. Novels, such as *The Pearl, Of Mice and Men, To Kill a Mockingbird,* many of the same ones you read in school, are examined for these bullying issues, which might go undetected. For example, in *The Christmas Carol,* social class discrimination and bullying those who are weak can be addressed. The site provides useful charts and excellent examples of this type of curriculum infusion.

Forgan and Gonzales-DeHass (2004, p. 26), as cited by McNamara (2007), provide the following literature synopsis on the infusion of social skills training into the curriculum.

- One approach for overcoming the dilemma of either teaching academics or social skills is to infuse social skills instruction into the academic curriculum (Sugai & Lewis, 1996) and literacy instruction in particular (Bauer & Balius, 1995; Forness & Kavale, 1996; Anderson, 2000; Cartledge & Kiarie, 2001; Gresham, Watson, & Skinner, 2001).
- By infusing social skills training into the academic curriculum, students receive vastly more time devoted to social skills training than when these programs are offered as an isolated area of instruction, which traditionally amounts to a total of 30 hours or less (Forness & Kavale, 1996; Gresham et al., 2001).
- Training that is divorced from meaningful settings may result in a lack of transfer of social skills. Literature activities offer an ideal opportunity to teach skills through a medium that can be perceived as meaningful to students' lives (Korineck & Popp, 1997).
- Literacy affords students the natural tendency to read a book in search of answers, and teachers can use children's literature books to help students learn to solve problems and enhance self-concept. Bibliotherapy allows students to see that they are not the only ones to encounter such problems and learn that there is more than one solution to a problem. It helps them discuss the problem or freely create a constructive course of action to solve it (Alex, 1993).
- *Working Together: Building Children's Social Skills Through the Literature* allows students the opportunity to relate with a folk literature character so that skills are presented in a natural context of literacy rather than as a separate entity; this program has been successfully used to increase the social skills of middle school adolescents with behavior disorders (Blake, Wang, Cartledge, & Gardner, 2000).

Summary

This chapter provided information on instructional approaches and techniques that will allow teachers to modify the school-wide bully prevention program for students with disabilities. PBS programs, collaborative teaching approaches, and DI were discussed, with a focus on ways to apply them to bullying.

TEST YOURSELF

1. What are the major components of PBS?
2. What are the essential elements of BP-PBS?
3. What are the defining characteristics of collaboration?
4. What are the coteaching models?
5. How can they be utilized in a bully prevention program?
6. How would you differentiate content?
7. How would you differentiate process?
8. How would you differentiate products?
9. How would you differentiate learning environment?
10. What is an anchoring activity?

Books on Bullying (For Students)

www.amazon.com/Best-Sellers-Books-Childrens-Bullies-Issues
www.best-childrens-books.com/childrens-books-about-bullying Search for Steve Barack's Best Children's Books.
http://voices.yahoo.com/bullying
http://www.chicagonow.com Search for the article "Anti-Bullying: Reading Recommendations for Children and Teens." This provides a direct link to amazon.com if you want to purchase a book.
www.scholastic.com Search for children's books on bullying.
www.crisisprevention.com/stopbullying
www.adl.org/education/curriculum_connections/winter 2005 Search for the article "Using Children's Literature to Increase Empathy and Help Students Cope With Bullying." It provides a thorough, annotated bibliography.
www.publishersweekly.com Search for bullying resources.
www.reading.org This is the International Reading Association's website. Search for "A Review of Books About Bullying."
www.education.wisc.edu/ccbc/books/detaillistbook This is the website for the library of the School of Education at the University of Wisconsin at Madison. Search for "Thick-Skinned, Thin-Skinned, the Skin I'm In" for a selected bibliography of books about bullying, teasing, relational aggression, and school violence.

Useful Websites for Dealing With Bullying

www.stopbullying.gov
This is the U.S. Department of Health and Human Services' national Bullying Prevention Program. This provides resources for families, educators, and the community.
www.abilitypath.org
This is a useful website for parents of children with special needs. You can download their excellent report on bullying, *Walk a Mile in Their Shoes*.
www.p12.NYSED.gov/dignityact/
This is the website for New York State's DASA. In addition to describing the act, it provides valuable resources on bullying and harassment as well as social-emotional learning.
www.pacer.org/bullying
The PACER Center is a parent training and information center for families of children and youth with all disabilities from birth through 21. In 2006, they launched their bullying prevention programs, Pacer Kids and Pacer Teens.
www.ncld.org
This is the site for the National Center on Learning Disabilities. In addition to providing invaluable information for families and teachers on specific learning disabilities, they also have a number of resources on bullying. These are applicable for a wide variety of students with disabilities.
www.cec.sped.org
The Council for Exceptional Children is a well-established organization providing educators and families with an incredible number of resources, including many on bullying and special education.
www.cyberbullying.us
This is the home of the Cyberbullying Research Center. They provide extensive information on the topic, including blogs, publications, and resources for families and educators. It is a clearinghouse for information on cyberbullying and is constantly being updated.
www.nea.org/neabullyfree/
This is the website of the NEA. It provides information on their Bully Free program and very useful information for paraprofessionals regarding bullying prevention.

www.pbis.org

This is the website for the Office of Special Education Program's (OSEP) Technical Assistance Center on Positive Behavioral Intervention and Support. It provides an excellent example of how to integrate a PBS program with a bullying prevention program. They provide a wealth of information, including research, support, and videos. They also provide lesson plans.

www.specialolympics.org

This is the website for the Special Olympics. It addresses issues related to bullying and diversity as well as celebrating the accomplishments of athletes with IDD.

www.bestbuddies.com

The Best Buddies program was initiated by the Special Olympics and pairs middle- and high-school students with individuals with IDD. They provide information on how to start such a program in your school.

The purpose of this list was to provide a quick reference to excellent resources on bullying. If you have time and want to explore more, you can search the list below.

www.cumbavac.org/bullying-violence-vandalism.htm

This is a long list of websites, lesson plans, and classroom activities developed by the Cumberland County AVA Center staff. The staff evaluates the content and provides a rating.

www.pbskids.org/itsmylife/friends/bullies

PBS Kids provides a wide variety of programs, and these focus on establishing friendships and dealing with bullies.

www.antibullying.net/resourceswithlinks.htm

This website lists innumerable websites on bullying and connects you directly to them.

www.kzoo.edu/psych/stop-bullying/index/html

This is an interesting website. It was developed by students at Kalamazoo College's Stop Bullying Project. The students evaluate the content, and it is frequently updated.

www.differentiationcentral.com

This is the website of the Institute on Academic Diversity at the Curry School of Education, University of Virginia. It is the most thorough site on the topic.

References

AbilityPath. (2011). *Walk a mile in their shoes.* Retrieved June 7, 2012, from www.abilitypath.org

Alberto, P. A., & Troutman, A. C. (2013). Applied behavior analysis for teachers (9th ed.). Upper Saddle River, NJ: Pearson.

Alex, N. K. (1993). Bibliotherapy (Report NO.EDO-CS-93–05). Bloomington: Indiana University, Office of Educational Research and Improvement (ERIC).

Anderson, P. L. (2000). Using literature to teach social skills to adolescents with LD. *Interventions in School and Clinic, 35,* 271–279.

Atlas, R. S., & Pepler, D. J. (1998). Observation of bullying in the classroom. *The Journal of Educational Research, 92,* 86–97.

Bandura, A. (2002). Growing primacy of human agency in adaptation and change in the electronic era. *European Psychologist, 7,* 2–16.

Bandura, A., & Walters, R. (1963). *Social learning and personality development.* NY: Holt, Rinehart & Winston.

Bassity, K. & Owens, D. (n.d.). The who, what and how of paraprofessionals: Using these instructional supports effectively. Retrieved November 10, 2012, from www.education.com

Bauer, M. S., & Balius, F. A. (1995). Storytelling: Integrating therapy and curriculum for students with serious emotional disturbances. *Teaching Exceptional Children, 27*(2), 24–28.

Bellmore-Merrick UFSD. (n.d.). Retrieved February 11, 2013, from www.bellmore-merrick.k12.ny.us

Bender, W. N. (2007). *Differentiating instruction for students with learning disabilities: Best practices for general and special educators.* Thousand Oaks, CA: Corwin Press.

Best Buddies. (n.d.). Retrieved March 20, 2013, from www.bestbuddies.com

Blake, C., Wang, W., Cartledge, G., & Gardner, R. (2000). Middle school students with serious emotional disturbances serve as social skills trainers and reinforcers for peers with SED. *Behavioral Disorders, 25,* 280–290.

Broer, S. M., Doyle, M. B., Giangreco, M. F. (2005). Perspectives of students with intellectual disabilities about their experiences with paraprofessional support. *Exceptional Children, 71*(4), 415–430.

Carter, B., & Spencer, V. (2006). The fear factor. Bullying and students with disabilities. *International Journal of Special Education, 21*(1), 11–23.

Cartledge, G., & Klarie, M. W. (2001). Learning social skills through literature for children and adolescents. *Exceptional Children, 55,* 298–302.

Chapman, C., & Gregory, G. H. (2007). *Differentiated instructional strategies: One size doesn't fit all* (2nd ed.). Thousand Oaks, CA: Corwin Press.

Coloroso, B. (2002). *The bully, the bullied, and the bystander.* NY: William Morrow.

Craig, W. M., & Pepler, D. J. (2003). Identify and target risk for involvement in bullying and victimization. *Canadian Journal of Psychology, 48,* 577–82.

Crothers, L. M., & Kolbert, J. B. (2004). Comparing middle school teachers' and students' views on bullying and anti-bullying interventions. *Journal of School Violence, 31*(1), 17–32.

Cyberbullying Research Center. (n.d.). Retrieved September 1, 2012, from www.cyberbullying.us

Dignity for All Students Act (DASA). (2012). Retrieved, July 20, 2012, from www.p12.nysed.gov/dignityact

Drake, J. A., Price, J. H., & Telljohann, S. K. (2003). The nature and extent of bullying at school. *Journal of School Health, 73*(5), 173–180.

Espelage, D. L., & Swearer, S. M. (Eds.). (2004). *Bullying in American schools: A social-ecological perspective on prevention and intervention.* Mahwah, NJ: Lawrence Erlbaum.

Forgan, J. W., & Gonzales-DeHass, A. (2004). How to infuse social skills training into literacy instruction. *Teaching Exceptional Children, 36,* 24–30.

Forness, S. R., & Kavale, K. A. (1996). Treating social skills deficits in children with learning disabilities: A meta-analysis of the research. *Learning Disability Quarterly, 19,* 2–13.

Friend, M., & Cook, L. (2013). *Interactions: Collaboration skills for school professionals.* Upper Saddle River, NJ: Pearson.

Garrity, C., Jens, K., Porter, W., Sager, N., & Short-Camilla, C. (2004). *Bully-Proofing your school.* Longmont, CO: Sopris West. (Original work published 2000)

Giangreco, M. F. (2010). One-to-one paraprofessionals for students with disabilities in inclusive classrooms: Is conventional wisdom wrong? *Intellectual and Developmental Disabilities, 48*(1), 1–13.

Good, C. P., McIntosh, K., & Geitz, C. (2011). Integrating bullying into a school-wide positive behavior support. *Teaching Exceptional Children, 44*(1), 48–50.

Gresham, F. M., Watson, T. S., & Skinner, C. H. (2001). FBA: Principles, procedures, and future directions. *School Psychology Review, 30,* 156–172.

Hanish, L., & Guerra N. G. (2000). Predictors of peer victimization among urban minority youth. *Social Development, 6,* 521–543.

Heinrichs, R. (2003). Perfect targets: Asperger syndrome and bullying, practical solutions for surviving the social world. Shawnee Mission, KS: Autism Asperger.

Hermantown School District, Hermantown MN. (2010). *Paraprofessional handbook.* Retrieved August 15, 2012, from www.hermantown.k12.mn.us

Kim, Y., & Leventhal, B. (2008). Bullying and suicide: A review. *Interactional Journal of Adolescent Medicine and Health, 20*(2), 133–154.

Klomek, A. B., Sourander, A., & Gould, M. S. (2011). Bullying and suicide. *Psychiatric Times, 28,* 2.

Korinek, L., & Popp, P. A. (1997). Collaborative mainstream integration of social skills with academic instruction. *Preventing School Failure, 41,* 148–152.

Lumsden, L. (2002). *Preventing bullying.* Retrieved September 10, 2012, from http://ericass.uncg.edu/virtuallit/bullying/1068html.ED144

Mastropieri, M. A., & Scruggs, T. E. (1998). Enhancing school success with mnemonic strategies. Retrieved May 10, 2012, from www.ldonline.org/article/5912

McNamara, B. E. (2007). *Learning disabilities: Bridging the gap between research and classroom practice.* Upper Saddle River, NJ: Pearson.

McNamara, B. E., & McNamara, F. J. (1997). *Keys to dealing with bullies.* Hauppauge, NY: Barron Education.

McLesky, J., & Waldron, N. L. (2002). Inclusion and school change: Teachers' perception regarding curricular and instructional strategies. *Teacher Education and Special Education, 25,* 41–54.

Mishna, F. (2003). Learning disabilities and bullying: Double jeopardy. *Journal of Learning Disabilities, 36*(4), 336–347.

National Education Association (NEA). (2010). Perspectives on bullying. Retrieved November, 7, 2012, from www.nea.org/home/neabullyfree.html

NICHCY. (2012). Categories of disability under IDEA. Retrieved September 14, 2012, from http://nichcy.org

Office of Civil Rights (OCR) Department of Education. (1989). *The civil rights of students with disabilities under Section 504 of the Rehabilitation Act of 1973.* Washington, DC: Author.

Olweus, D. (1993). *Bullying at school: What we know and what we can do.* Cambridge, MA: Blackwell.

Olweus, D. (1994). Annotation: Bullying at school: Basic facts and effects of a school-based intervention program. *Journal of Child Psychology and Psychiatry, 35,* 1171–1190.

Olweus, D. (2003).A profile of bullying and schools. *Educational Leadership, 60*(6), 12–17.

Olweus, D., & Limber, S. (1999). *Blueprints for violence prevention: Bullying prevention program.* Boulder: Institute of Behavioral Science, University of Colorado.

OSEP Technical Assistance Center on Positive Behavioral Interventions and Supports. (2003). *Schoolwide PBS.* Retrieved November 5, 2012, from www.pbis.org/english/Schoolwide_PBS.htm

Mercer, C. D., Mercer, A. R., & Pullen, P. C. (2011). Teaching students with learning problems (8th ed.). Upper Saddle River, NJ: Pearson.

PACER Center. (2003). Pacer Center's bullying prevention project. Retrieved November 20, 2012, from www.pacer.org

Raskaukas, J., & Modell, S. (2011). Modifying anti-bullying programs to include students with disabilities. *Teaching Exceptional Children, 44*(1), 60–67.

Rose, C. A., Espelage, D. L., & Monda-Amaya, L. E. (2009). Bullying and victimization rates among students in general and special education: A comparative analysis. *Educational Psychology, 29*(7), 761–776.

Rose, C. A., Monda-Amaya, L. E., & Espelage, D. L. (2011). Bullying perpetration and victimization in special education: A review of the literature. *Remedial and Special Education, 32,* 114–130.

Ross, S. W., & Horner, R. H. (2009). Bully prevention in positive behavior support. *Journal of Applied Behavior Analysis, 42*(4), 747–759.

Ross, S. W., Horner, R. H., & Stiller, B. (2011). *Bully prevention in positive behavior support.* Retrieved October 12, 2012, from www.pbs.org

Salend, S. J. (2008). *Creating inclusive classrooms: Effective and reflective practices.* Upper Saddle River, NJ: Pearson.

Sugai, A. A., & Lewis, T. J. (1996). Preferred and promising practices for social skills instruction. *Focus on Exceptional Children, 29,* 1–16.

Siebecker, S., Wang, C., Maag, J. W., Siebecher, A. B., & Frerichs, L. J. (2012). Understanding the bullying dynamic among students in general and special education. *Journal of School Psychology, 50*(4), 503–520.

Special Olympics. (n.d.). Retrieved March 20, 2013, from www.specialoympics .org

Spense Fact Sheet. (2001). Study of personnel needs in special education. Retrieved October 10, 2012, from www.spense.org

Stop Bullying Now. (n.d.). Retrieved May 17, 2012, from www.stopbullying .gov

Tomilson, C. A. (1999). *The differentiated classroom: Responding to the needs of all learners.* Alexandria, VA: ASCD.

United States Department of Education. (2010). Retrieved from www .stopbullying.gov

United States Department of Health and Human Services. (2010). Tips for paraeducators. Retrieved from www.samhsa.org

University of Maryland Medical Center (UMMC). (2011). Retrieved November 20, 2012, from www.umm.edu

Walker, H. M., Horner, R. H., Sugai, G., Bullis, M., Sprague, J. R., Bricker, D., & Kaufman, M. J. (1996). Integrated approaches to preventing antisocial behavior patterns among school-aged children and youth. *Journal of Emotional and Behavioral Disorders, 4*(4), 194–209.

Weiss, M. P., & Lloyd, J. W. (2003). Conditions for co-teaching: Lessons learned from a case study. *Teacher Education and Special Education, 26,* 27–41.

Will, J. D., & Neufeld, P. (2002). Taking appropriate action. *Principal Leadership, 3,* 51–54.

Wilson, D. (2004). The interface of school climate and school connectedness and relationships with aggression and victimization. *Journal of School Health, 74*(7), 293, 303.

Young, J., Ne'eman, A., & Gelser, S. (2011). Bullying and students with disabilities. *White House Conference on Bullying Prevention.* Retrieved August 27, 2012, from www.ncd.gov/publications/2011/March92011

Index

Figures are indicated by f following the page number.

CORWIN
A SAGE Company

The Corwin logo—a raven striding across an open book—represents the union of courage and learning. Corwin is committed to improving education for all learners by publishing books and other professional development resources for those serving the field of PreK–12 education. By providing practical, hands-on materials, Corwin continues to carry out the promise of its motto: **"Helping Educators Do Their Work Better."**